Praise for *The Pow* ... *dmillion*

"Developing a meditation practice can seem mysterious, difficult, or overly rigorous. Edward approaches meditation like a friend and invites you into the practice with ease, simplicity, and warmth. Practical, down to earth, yet embedded in the classic tradition, Edward illuminates the Power of Meditation and develops the practices that help you discover that power for yourself."

—PETRA WELDES, SENIOR MINISTER, CENTER FOR SPIRITUAL LIVING, DALLAS

"What a wonderful book! With clear and direct writing, Edward Viljoen has brought forth an illuminated guide for establishing a meditation practice or teaching others to do so. Edward's reflections on the practices meaningful to him and on his unfolding experiences and realizations are windows into the deep process, the inner landscape and what it takes to cultivate stillness, watching, and listening. Knowing Edward, I have always marveled at the person he is. Seeing him now in the light of this book, I appreciate how beautifully his practice expresses through him. What is revealed here is the richness and value of a spiritual life that has meditation, insight, wisdom, and love at its center."

—DR. KATHY HEARN, FOUNDER AND SENIOR MINISTER,
PACIFIC CHURCH OF RELIGIOUS SCIENCE, SAN DIEGO

"Edward Viljoen has created a defining work on the power of meditation. Not only does he give us a compelling rationale on the depth of experience possible through this ancient spiritual practice, but he also brings meditation to life with his understanding of its breadth of expression and the vast possibilities it offers to the awakening spirit. I love this book!"

—DR. JOHN B. WATERHOUSE, PRESIDENT, CENTERS FOR SPIRITUAL LIVING

"What a lovely book. This is an honest discussion of the act of meditation. By sharing his personal experience he brings home the truth that meditation is something we have to do, not something we have to understand. His experience with resistance, attachment, and surrender are beautifully expressed throughout. I found The Power of Meditation to be the perfect balance of gentle guidance and 'just do it.' Edward shares his deep wisdom clearly born out of experience and practice. He has indeed contributed to the movement of peace on our planet."

—JULIE INTERRANTE, MA, AUTHOR OF *THE POWER OF A BROKEN-OPEN HEART*

"There are many books that talk about meditating—the difference with The Power of Meditation is that it gives the reader permission and support to find the way that works best for them. Through his own path of exploring various techniques of meditating, Edward Viljoen shares his insights like a trusted coach and friend in helping the reader choose techniques and practices that are easy to use. Even the simple idea of just committing to ten minutes a day at the same time in the same place, gave me the inspiration to re-commit to my own practice!"

—KAREN DRUCKER, MUSICIAN AND AUTHOR OF LET GO OF THE SHORE

"Edward Viljoen has written a passionate and compassionate guide to the challenges—and benedictions—of looking within and cultivating what is perhaps the essential ingredient in an authentic life: self-awareness. In a voice that is full of warmth and wisdom, he teaches us how to be both receptive and responsive to life and to what it calls for from us, and how to practice, as he puts it, 'living wide awake.' I heartily recommend it."

—GREGG MICHAEL LEVOY, AUTHOR OF
CALLINGS: FINDING AND FOLLOWING AN AUTHENTIC LIFE

"Meditation can change the very structure of your brain by building new neuropathways to the centers of peace, while calming those centers of agitation and distraction. If you use this book, that can happen to you. Dr. Viljoen understands meditation from the inside-out because he practices what he writes—'he gets it' and he has developed a very workable everyday guide to finding the reservoirs of strength within you. If you can breathe, you can meditate, and this book teaches you how, even if you think you never could."

—DR. WILLIAM K. LARKIN, DIRECTOR, APPLIED NEUROSCIENCE INSTITUTE

"Creatively blending the guidance of the ancient Bhagavad Gita with his fresh and modern approach, Dr. Viljoen brings the process of meditation to life in a new way. He is a deep and authentic teacher disguised as a friend sharing stories, offering wisdom and encouragement on every page."

—AUGUST GOLD, COAUTHOR OF
THE PRAYER CHEST and MULTIPLY YOUR BLESSINGS

"Edward Viljoen's The Power of Meditation beautifully helps the reader dissolve any resistance to one of the greatest spiritual practices of all time. Slowing down the mind and creating a peace-filled harbor of balance, breath, and connectivity has perhaps never been more compellingly offered in book form before. The book's insightful instruction to begin a practice or revise an old one will have you returning to its pages again and again for inspiration."

—DAVID AULT, AUTHOR OF *WHERE REGRET CANNOT FIND ME*

"Dr. Edward Viljoen provides a wonderful, step-by-step way to use the powerful spiritual tool of meditation. Whether you are new to meditation or are seasoned in the practice, The Power of Meditation has ideas and techniques to support you in making this practice part of your daily routine. With his trademark clarity, Dr. Viljoen gives us a book that is accessible, informative, and profoundly enjoyable!"

—JUDY MORLEY, PH.D., RSCP, DIRECTOR OF COMMUNICATIONS, CENTERS FOR SPIRITUAL LIVING, DENVER

"Edward Viljoen is a wonderful teacher who has the ability to make the complex seem simple. The Power of Meditation will touch your heart, inspire your soul, and empower you on your spiritual journey in a beautiful way."

—MIKE ROBBINS, AUTHOR OF *BE YOURSELF, EVERYONE ELSE IS ALREADY TAKEN*

"If you are new to the practice of meditation, or if you have been meditating for years, Edward Viljoen's The Power of Meditation promises to be a remarkable guide to accompany you on the inward journey. Like a comfortable friend or devoted coach, Viljoen shares his love of meditation and generously offers his experience as a fellow seeker. The book presents a variety of techniques for courting the presence, but perhaps even more valuable are Viljoen's profound insights and mindful questions that can stir an awakening to the life within and rekindle an appreciation of the peace and wisdom found in the present moment. Simple, clear, and thoughtful, this book will help the reader to ignite the power of meditation and keep the fire aglow."

—CLAUDIA ABBOTT, EDITOR OF *SCIENCE OF MIND* MAGAZINE

"I've known Edward Viljoen for almost twenty years and he never ceases to amaze me with his depth of compassion, wisdom, and peacefulness. I believe all this comes from his personal commitment to all kinds of mindfulness practices. If he is an example of a person who meditates, then we all should read this book."

—KATHIANNE LEWIS, D.D., SENIOR MINISTER, CENTER FOR SPIRITUAL LIVING, SEATTLE

"*In our fast-paced, high-tech, low-touch society, where 'making it happen' and 'getting it done' is the common language of the ambitious, Edward Vijoen strikes a chime that confronts America's busyness with a loud silence. The Power of Meditation opens a window from antiquity that blows in a breath of fresh air for the seeker looking to trade in the 'rush hour rat race' for a 'hush hour life break.' The meditation practices that he offers in this book are so inclusive that even the most skeptical will find herself hooked in the stillness. Edward has masterfully introduced us to the 'new action' that is sure to inspire and empower people to design and live the lives of their dreams.*"

—KEVIN KITRELL ROSS, HOST OF *DESIGN YOUR LIFE* ON UNITY ONLINE RADIO, SPIRITUAL DIRECTOR, UNITY OF SACRAMENTO, AND AUTHOR OF *LIVING THE DESIGNER LIFE*

"*Dr. Edward Viljoen's book,* The Power of Meditation, *is an exciting and enticing path to accessing a larger part of who you are. His clear guidance to quieting your active mind will take you beyond surface thinking with an 'attitude of watchfulness' to discovery and understanding from your enlightened self. His time-tested techniques for meditation will free you to be able to make the right choices for your life from an expanded, peaceful awareness. This book is a life-changer for your greater good!*"

—REV. CHRISTIAN SORENSEN, D.D., SEASIDE CENTER FOR SPIRITUAL LIVING

THE POWER OF
MEDITATION

JEREMY P. TARCHER/PENGUIN
A Member of Penguin Group (USA)
New York

The

POWER of
MEDITATION

An Ancient Technique to Access
Your Inner Power

EDWARD VILJOEN

JEREMY P. TARCHER/PENGUIN
Published by the Penguin Group
Penguin Group (USA), 375 Hudson Street,
New York, New York 10014, USA

USA · Canada · UK · Ireland · Australia
New Zealand · India · South Africa · China

Penguin Books Ltd, Registered Offices:
80 Strand, London WC2R 0RL, England
For more information about the Penguin Group visit penguin.com

All references to the Bhagavad Gita are from *The Bhagavad Gita*, translated by
Eknath Easwaran, founder of the Blue Mountain Center of Meditation,
copyright © 1985, 2007; reprinted by permission of Nilgiri Press,
P.O. Box 256, Tomales, CA 94971, www.easwaran.org

Most Tarcher/Penguin books are available at special quantity discounts for
bulk purchase for sales promotions, premiums, fund-raising, and educational needs.
Special books or book excerpts also can be created to fit specific
needs. For details, write: Special.Markets@us.penguingroup.com.

Library of Congress Cataloging-in-Publication Data

Viljoen, Edward.
The power of meditation : an ancient technique
to access your inner power / Edward Viljoen.
p.   cm.
ISBN 978-0-399-16261-9
1. Meditation.   I. Title.
BL627.V55   2013   2013016744
204'. 35—dc23

Printed in the United States of America
3   5   7   9   10   8   6   4

BOOK DESIGN BY EMILY S. HERRICK

CONTENTS

INTRODUCTION

Every author of a book about meditation has their own point of view, their own reason for teaching about meditation, and why it has worked for them. A doctor might write about meditation as a method for lowering blood pressure, a therapist might write about meditation as a tool to calm the nerves, and an athlete might write about how meditation can help improve athletic ability.

My point of view is to teach meditation as spiritual practice, as it has been used for centuries in all of the world's wisdom traditions. You can be of any (or no) spiritual or religious background to use this book, and the techniques I teach here can be used with no spiritual motivation whatsoever. However, this book can open you up to an awakening of what meditation is, why it is important, and some practical ways you can begin—immediately—to practice meditation here and now. You don't need a lofty spiritual goal, you only need to bring your desire to learn and have a willingness to try. My words in this book won't take the place of you actually sitting, but I hope this book can inspire you to do so.

You'll notice throughout this book that I reference the Bhagavad Gita, which I've found to be one of the most beautiful spiritual texts ever written. The Gita has been a guide for me in my journey of learning to meditate, and so I've included passages and points from the Gita for you as well. (If you want to explore the Gita more, check out my e-book *The Bhagavad Gita for Beginners*, which is a simplified version of this ancient text.)

What follows is a simple guidebook that can be used by anybody who seeks to begin the art of meditation and discover the gifts that meditation can bring. In addition to specific teaching on meditation, I will share some of my personal journey of teaching what I most needed to learn and the sometimes surprising insights and unexpected revelations that came as a result. I think I studied meditation largely because I wanted so many things: wisdom, personal power, practical spiritual skills, and to finally, actually be— and appear to be—spiritual. In the process, and to my frustration and later to my joy, I achieved very few of my original goals—or at least not in the form I had in mind.

Wisdom, I came to see, has less to do with knowing information and techniques, and more to do with a passionate interest in reality, which some say is utterly unknowable. Nevertheless, the interest in exploring what is real both inside and outside opened the door to an infinity of ideas and awarenesses without which I began to wonder how I had ever managed. The personal power and self-determination I was reaching for gave way to something less tangible, something that I can best describe as a felt sense of being at home in this life. Instead of gaining control over the world, I discovered the power and beauty of what is happening right now and the sweet (and potent) options that became available to me to help and love the world when I started to observe life with a little more honesty and accuracy.

Observing life through meditation with less "unnecessary added meaning" to what was happening inside and outside allowed reality to come into clearer focus.

It was in the practice of meditation that my initial goal became gently undone—not so much in a flash of insight but more in gradual steps of accepting what is, who I am, and the nature of things. My view of others softened and I began to appreciate the sincere desire I saw in them to learn something powerful to help their own lives. I began to notice my growing respect for the courage it took the average person to navigate their lives, and I found myself falling in love with people in a new way.

"Spiritual," for me, began to mean something more down to earth, and meditation was allowing me to see spirituality everywhere. I began to have a down-to-earth look at life and cultivated a what-you-see-is-what-you-get curiosity about people, events, and things. This in turn opened the door to seeing how truly magical everything and everyone is without my help. In Stephen Greenblatt's *The Swerve*, his summary of Lucrecian worldview reminded me of a state of mind I came upon as a result of practicing meditation. I can describe it best as a kind of unhooking from cultural concepts, or an openness to reality, or a willingness to question everything previously believed.

He writes:

> But nothing—from our own species to the planet on which we live to the sun that lights our days—lasts forever. Only the atoms are immortal. In a universe so constituted, Lucretius argued, there is no reason to think that the earth or its inhabitants occupy a central place, no reason to set humans apart from all other animals, no hope of bribing or appeasing the gods, no place for religious fanaticism, no call for ascetic self-denial, no justification for dreams of

limitless power or perfect security, no rationale for wars of conquest or self-aggrandizement, no possibility of triumphing over nature, no escape from the constant making and unmaking and remaking of forms. On the other side of anger at those who either peddled false visions of security or incited irrational fears of death, Lucretius offered a feeling of liberation and the power to stare down what had once seemed so menacing. What human beings can and should do, he wrote, is to conquer their fears, accept the fact that they themselves and all the things they encounter are transitory, and embrace the beauty and the pleasure of the world.*

There was a time when words like these may have been disconcerting to me based on the worldview I had inherited about the central importance of humanity and the meaning of life. Now, rather than leaving me feeling hopeless and ineffectual, these words, and ideas like them, draw me closer to watching reality to discover what it is, really, to look at and appreciate impermanence, to let myself be drawn to what is mine to do, and, most important, how to love what is before me as consistently as I can.

....

* Stephen Greenblatt, *The Swerve: How the World Became Modern* (New York: W. W. Norton & Company, 2011), p. 6.

I learned this through meditation. I learned not to shy away from terrifying thoughts and not to reject concepts I disagreed with, and to be at peace with the world as much as I could.

Meditation gave me a feeling of liberation and the strength to be present with life. My invitation to you is that you be your own testing ground, your own experiment and proof so that you do not have to depend on the testimony of others about what meditation is and does. In Richard Bach's *Illusions: The Adventures of a Reluctant Messiah* is this advice:

> *Your only obligation in any lifetime is to be true to yourself. Being true to anyone else or anything else is not only impossible, but the mark of a fake messiah.**

I can say with confidence that before I meditated, I didn't know which me to be true to. So loud and frenzied was the content of my thought that I hadn't really met myself well enough to know if I *could* be true to me. It sometimes seemed to me that there were inside my own head multiple versions of myself, sometimes at odds with each

* Richard Bach, *Illusions: The Adventures of a Reluctant Messiah* (New York: Random House, 1989), p. 47.

other, competing for prominence in decision making. With the practice of sitting in meditation regularly, I began to be able to "watch" the antics of these internal characters and listen to their voices and begin to sort out what was valuable and what was not. I doubt that I have fully met all there is to meet in me and all there is to meet in the people around me, but I'm excited that there appears to be a way to do that. To sit and let reality reveal itself is among the greatest blessings in my life.

So now, read . . . and then sit. There is nothing more quietly revolutionary than to sit in silence. That—the sitting and all that it brings—is the power of meditation.

THE POWER OF MEDITATION

On this path effort never goes to waste, and there is no failure. Even a little effort toward spiritual awareness will protect you from the greatest fear.

BHAGAVAD GITA 2:40

What Is Meditation?

The term "meditation" is as broad in definition as is the term "art." Both include a wide range of practices, styles, and purposes. For instance, art can be engaged in for therapeutic reasons, or for fun and recreation, or for many other reasons. Art has different disciplines, each with its distinct schools of thought, media, and tools. Accomplished artists in one discipline may not exhibit skillfulness in another, and may not even understand the methods of a different media.

In the same way, meditation is different things to different people. There are certain meditative practices that work better for me, practices I respond to and understand better. By "practice," I mean the daily method I use to meditate. If I were a watercolor artist, I might say watercolor was my preferred medium and I might not care to waste my time chiseling away at a marble block to reveal a hidden statue therein. As a watercolorist, when I spoke about my art and the benefits, goals, and methods of its practice, I would be talking in a language that other watercolorists understood. Although there would be crossover points universal to all artists, I would have found my niche, my way, and my art. I may have even dabbled with other forms of art in the journey to discover what fits best, or I might have been one of those duck-to-water artists that picks it up and simply knows how to do it.

Similarly, when I talk about meditation, I'm talking about *my* best practice and I tend, sometimes, to talk as if it is the only way. I know this isn't the case, and I think what is coming through is my enthusiasm for what I have developed in my understanding of what meditation can be for me. I did dabble with all kinds of practices, and a little of everything I encountered along the way has lingered in what has become my practice today. I have developed a multifaceted approach in which three distinct tools form the meditative practice I use, and that I teach to others:

MINDFULNESS PRACTICES: in which we become absorbed in a purposefully chosen activity

SITTING PRACTICES: in which we reduce the use of mental and physical resources as much as possible by sitting still and silently

CREATIVE PRACTICES: in which we use some device such as journaling, observing, or focusing on an inspirational passage

You'll find examples of, and instructions for, all three of these main practices in this book.

Within these three groups, the practices that give access to this natural state of inner peace that meditation brings are varied. Some meditation practices include movement, eating mindfully, thoughtfully conducted ceremonial actions, counting beads to keep track of recited phrases, and so much more. The power of meditation is similar to the power of poetry, in that it has the ability to open doors of understanding and awareness that remain closed in ordinary states of mind.

What method you use to get there seems less important than that you go on the journey. To think that there is only one way to meditate is not accurate, and it isn't all mental, it is an integration of thoughts, feeling, sensation, body, mind, and movement. You may discover, or invent, a method that isn't described in this or any other book, and you may realize that you already know the way to your inner world of peace. Moreover, you may also discover as I did that meditation is not confined to the time spent in an activity; it becomes an approach to life and affects the way you think about your place in the scheme of things, the meaning of your life, your beliefs and aspirations, and so much more. For this reason, in this book I write not only about specific exercises you can try but also about the bigger picture of my changed worldview that came about as a result of meditating.

What Releases the Power That Is Meditation?

Consistency in practice does. Meditation requires practice, and with a schedule of regular sitting, you will develop momentum, and that momentum will take you beyond what this or any other book can impart to you. There is an unpredictable and beautiful power that can be released in your life through sitting in meditation.

I will be offering various suggestions about techniques and practices as I describe my own journey. Give my suggested techniques and practices a try. What I hope to convey most of all is that there is an ideal way for you to meditate, and as you discover what works and what doesn't, it will likely lead you to your own experience of what was always in you: a profoundly peaceful place. And possibly your practice, as it has done for others, may result in dramatic life changes, or at least an increase in peace and quiet. I know it has for me.

Some of what I experienced I might have expected, but there have also been instances of unintended outcomes, unexpected growth, and changes in what I thought was permanent. I never imagined I would be the thing in this story that would change so dramatically.

Meditation opens a door between the world of how things appear to be and the world of how things really are. There are all kinds of ways to unlock and open this door, and frankly I like to use more than one method to do so. Nevertheless, meditation is one of those things that in my opinion is impossible to eliminate from the equation. Other spiritual practices such as inquiry, service, and study can and do lead to an expanded awareness of the nature of reality, yet it is important for me to notice that each of these is characterized by mental activity.

Although some forms of meditation employ active mental strategies, creativity, and imagination, the practice of being open, receptive, quiet, still, non-clinging has a substantially different tone or attitude. I am an avid advocate of sitting in stillness and silence as a necessary complement to practices that require analysis and reasoning. Yet, despite my keen support of this style of practice, I know that it isn't the only way, and indeed, it took me quite a lot of experimentation with methods, testing ways to still my mind, investigating whether or not I could ever achieve it, before I settled into a happier relationship with sitting and not-doing. So I acknowledge the value of and teach different forms of meditation and meditative-like practices, trying to match the method with the mindset of the student and trusting that all roads reach the same destination.

Why Meditate?

I once had the occasion to require the advice of a specialized attorney. The hourly rate for her services was exorbitant. Unfortunately, there was no one else who had the experience and successful history in the particular field of her expertise, and so the fee became worth paying. You can be certain that I arrived early for my hour appointment and that I spent time in advance preparing myself for the best use of the time. I didn't want to miss a thing, and so I brought along a printout of my questions and a notepad to take down every word she said. When she spoke, I paid attention, and what she told me to do, I did with faithfulness.

Think of meditation as time spent that way, time in which what happens is so valuable that it deserves your utmost attention and loyalty. The information gleaned from that attorney session had to be rendered into action for it to be truly valuable. I suppose I could have paid to sit in her office a second time and listened to her excellent advice all over again, and a third time and so on. But at some point, I had to do a thing or two with what she advised. A spiritual practice of a hundred percent meditation only, without complementary active practices, conjures in my mind an image of an automobile driving on the freeway with only one tire inflated.

The art of spiritual living, like a balanced diet, requires more than one form of nutrition, and benefits from a balanced approach in which the three types of meditation mentioned above form just one component of a larger picture. For example, selfless service to others (the practice of actively expressing loving-kindness), charitable contribution (the practice of sharing material wealth), expressing gratitude (the practice of acknowledging and appreciating), prayer (the practice of daily devotionals)—all in addition to meditation—are what I've found to be some of the basic minimum requirements of a spiritual life.

Of the components mentioned in the paragraph above, the first four are active. They consist of activities that can easily engage you and your mind. For this reason, they seem to have a stronger appeal and are more quickly adopted as spiritual practices among those beginning to explore what it means to lead a spiritual life. When people who are new to a spiritual way of life find themselves to be distressed by life's unexpected turns or when their minds are troubled with worry, they gravitate to something they can do, active remedies, perhaps because doing so contributes to them feeling confident that they are doing something useful for themselves and others.

In the beginning, they may have more difficulty establishing a meditation practice than they do learning to pray or committing to do some service in their community—possibly because their minds are busy, troubled, or worried and they don't yet know what to do with that. So sitting still may turn into a session of thinking about what is currently troubling them.

The problem with a spiritual life strategy that omits

meditation is that it can unintentionally be all action-oriented and self-directed. Now, that may not be such a bad thing if you understand your "self" well and you have thoroughly investigated your mind and its workings, and you are familiar with the hidden beliefs that sometimes inform your decisions. It is my experience that no one has fully and adequately explored that realm of self-awareness enough to say they no longer have to pay attention to it.

A spiritual life directed by intellect only is missing out on a richness of wisdom and peace that has always been inside us, possibly hidden below the surface activity of thought and ideas of who we are. Although a student will see terrific progress with whatever beginnings they make in learning to live a more spiritual life, with whatever spiritual tool they learn to use, and although they will see results in their own lives and in the lives of those around them rather quickly, without meditation it is possible that they will not have accessed a larger part of their being where intuitive wisdom, expansive thought, and enduring love can be drawn upon to lead them. They will likely reach a plateau, or bottom out, or lose interest in the spiritual way of living that they embarked on because something will seem to be missing.

A preacher once humorously explained the difference between prayer and meditation, saying that prayer is when you tell God what to do, and it is in meditation that God gets the only chance to tell *you* what to do. If prayer, study, service, contribution, and gratitude are active practices, meditation would not so much be passive as receptive. It is a practice of being available to something within you, something greater than your intellect alone. Think of it as a way to grant your intuition, or creative instinct, or higher self, or whatever you name that something, an opportunity to express itself in an uninterrupted way. Think of it as actively listening to someone you dearly love. Think of it as an audience with someone whom you admire and perhaps aspire to be like. Think of it as paying attention without force, rigidity, or intense effort.

The foundational components of each person's spiritual life will be different. I have taught the following spiritual practices to students for many years and can say from experience and with confidence that without some balance of these, or practices like these, it is difficult for meditation to advance beyond certain elementary levels. Service, study, contribution, acknowledgment, and prayer combined with meditation stir up a symbiotic balance of compassion, devotion, wisdom, gratitude, and intuition.

SERVICE to others is the act of purposefully putting the needs of others as first priority in terms of your time, attention, and resources. It means scheduling, on a regular basis, time to do something that contributes to the well-being, ease, and/or success of another, whether that is through an organization or on a one-on-one basis. Service connects us to other people and helps us see and draw near to those who are suffering so that we may, through our contribution of time or talent, contribute to the relief of their suffering so that they may be encouraged to pursue their own freedom.

STUDY, specifically spiritual study, is the practice of purposefully placing yourself in a learning environment in which you are exposed to ideas that did not originate in your own mind. It means actively seeking out elevating teachings and taking time to broaden your own base of understanding with thoughts that come from disciplines and cultures other than those you are already familiar with. Study develops wisdom and dissolves narrowness of thought. It grows tolerance for ambiguity and paradox, and contributes to a willingness to inquire and understand.

CONTRIBUTION is the act of establishing a regular practice of giving to either an organization or individuals who do work that you support. It means developing generosity of spirit and sharing a portion of what supply you have. In this regard, it is the companion practice to service. Whereas service contributes your gift of time, the practice of material contribution is about sharing your wealth. Each is an important component of spiritual life, and in my opinion, one does not substitute for the other.

ACKNOWLEDGMENT is the act of purposefully appreciating people, events, things, and creatures in your life. It means practicing to notice what is in your life and who is in your life, and articulating, either to them or to yourself, what you value about them and how they contribute to your life. Acknowledgment fosters an attitude of gratitude, and gratitude is the magical fuel that makes everything flow more beautifully.

PRAYER, like meditation, is a term that has a broad definition ranging from tradition to tradition. It deserves a more thorough description than what can meaningfully be fit into a paragraph, so for the purpose of this book I will simply say that prayer is good for you and should be practiced as regularly as brushing your teeth.

When I teach people to engage in these practices, inevitably they begin to experience a more settled frame of mind and become more aware of their relationship to everything in life. It is as if the various practices are paving the way for an even deeper experience, and meditation, I'm certain, is the way there.

2

BEGINNING TO MEDITATE

> When meditation is mastered, the mind is unwavering like the flame of a lamp in a windless place.
>
> BHAGAVAD GITA 6:19

Practical Preparation Tips

Among the most practically useful instructions for meditation is that of taking the necessary time to prepare for it. When a group gathers for a meditation class, for example, the individuals in the class come into the room in different states of mind. Some have been rushing to get to the class in time after a stressful day at work; others have spent a leisurely hour at a coffee shop or a walk around the lake, and so on. It takes a moment for the atmosphere in the room to settle down into the desired atmosphere for the class. For me, this shift in atmosphere, when it happens, feels tangible and I enjoy nothing more than sensing that moment when the group's attention is consolidated and re-focused from disparate points to the present moment and activity of the class.

To facilitate this shift, I ask the students to sit quietly in a moment of silence. I typically offer no more instruction than that. What follows is the gradual slowing down of small movements as people get their books and bags where they want them to be, throats clearing, chairs being adjusted, and eventually, like a gear moved into its cog, a moment comes when the stillness in the class arrives. Without announcing it, or directing it with instructions, the students and I find that moment naturally and easily, perhaps because it was always there, available in the room, needing only a moment of pause to become apparent.

If you arrive at your own meditation appointment in a rushed frame of mind, or even if you were doing something pleasurable just before, you might need an additional moment of pre-meditation preparation to shift gears, to settle down, to become situated, and to unhook from the pace of what you were engaged in.

One method I use is to do some basic seated stretches. The slow, intentional movements have the effect of inducing a quieter, introspective state of mind. Simply stretching each arm straight up for a moment or self-massaging of the scalp and/or hands, when repeated regularly, creates a conditioned response that can bring about the desired state of quietness more quickly. I begin to notice small movements in my body such as adjustments to posture, swallowing, or clearing my throat, and I imagine what it would be like if I didn't respond to their urges. What, I ask myself, would it be like if I just sat very, very still? Of course, if I need to scratch an itch, I will, but I have discovered that I can let an itch go on itching and be very peaceful without attending to it. And I have discovered that there is a natural quietness available to everyone, one that needs a little moment of pause to become available.

It's Not *That* You Close Your Eyes; It's *How* You Close Them

Closing your eyes for meditation seems like a simple act to accomplish. Nevertheless, there is a way to close your eyes that can contribute to an attitude of mindfulness and watchfulness. Instead of merely closing your eyes for meditation, purposefully give your attention to the process.

While your eyes are open, invite softness to the area of

your face around your eyes, which is just another way of saying relax your face around your eyes. To enhance your face's relaxation, let your jaw relax; and if you were holding your teeth together, let the bottom jaw drop without letting your mouth open. Notice how this conscious relaxation of specific parts of your face begins to affect other parts, like your throat and head and even your ears with sensations of relaxation.

Now you are beginning to be ready to let your eyes close. Letting your eyes close is different in attitude to closing your eyes, in that you imagine your eyelids are heavy in the way they can be when you are feeling very, very tired. The sensation is that the eyelids are being drawn together without any effort or thought. Imagine the lids gliding softly over your eyes, irresistibly drawn to each other, but without any urgency to arrive at the final closed position.

Notice how they are drawn to each other; in this way, you may become aware of the sensation of your eyelashes touching when the bottom and top lid become close enough, while at the same time you remain aware of the light coming in through the slit between your almost-closed eyelids. When you let your eyes close in this way, the lids may never fully close, and the softness with which you invited the process will establish you in a peacefully still frame of mind.

Unhelpful Expectations

Among the least helpful expectations I had about meditation was the idea that something otherworldly would happen. I also had acquired the thought that only after extended rigorous and dedicated practice could I expect to have that experience. I found it helpful to take these thoughts less seriously as my practice developed. Perhaps you too have an idea or expectation for what meditation should provide. In my case, these ideas and expectations got in the way of what the real experience had to offer. I have come to realize that different benefits result for different people, and going into a practice focused on any specific outcome seems less successful than giving the practice an opportunity to deliver to you what it will.

In my beginner's mind, I thought meditation would lead to profound insights about life and spiritual matters of the world around me. What I wasn't expecting was that the insights were about life *inside* of me. I noticed that I was both different and the same, before and after meditation. Different, in that meditation fostered in me a calmer mind with a stronger inclination to peaceful thoughts; the same, in that I am still capable of rushed, and sometimes inaccurate, thoughts. I am still prone to reactivity or unkind thoughts, but what has changed is that I am more tolerant of much that is in me, and with this tolerance has come an easier willingness not to be governed by it.

Perhaps I thought that through meditation I would wipe all that business away. Instead, something happened that I wasn't expecting. I began to see it—the *thinking*—and in that seeing was the insight I had been seeking: that I could observe my mind without reacting to everything in it.

Inner and Outer Order

On one of my visits to Bali, I had the opportunity to visit Dancing Dragon Cottages, a hotel designed and built according to Balinese and universal Feng Shui principles by Feng Shui author Karen Kingston and her Balinese husband, Rai. I made my pilgrimage to the hotel because I had received so much from Karen's book *Clear Your Clutter with Feng Shui*. Not only did I learn simple techniques to address chaos in my living space, but I also discovered ways to apply the same to my inner space.

The way I understand Feng Shui is that it deals with arranging things in a manner that is orderly and aesthetically pleasing. The Feng Shui practitioner draws upon training that sensitizes him or her to the invisible flow of energy and the right placement of things. The idea is that everything has its proper place, and when not in its proper place, it causes a disturbance in the rightness of things, an idea that I could immediately apply to my life, inner and outer.

When I look at a disorderly space now, I can see how items out of place cause a disruption. I sometimes look at my desk and ask the question, "What is out of order here?" Or, "What needs to be moved, relocated, or reordered for peace to be present?"

I also learned to begin the task of creating outer order in a mindful and humane pace, not attempting to fix an entirely disorderly household in an hour, but to be fully present and engaged in the act of clearing, cleaning, and rearranging one single drawer at a time. I learned to trust how one simple action could influence me in other areas and urge me on to further acts of orderliness. I learned how to avoid being overwhelmed by taking on tasks that were too big. In the same way, I learned to trust the simple act described above of mindfully closing my eyes and to have confidence that it would lead to deeper experiences of mindfulness.

Additionally, I began to notice the similarities between the effects of inner order and outer order. It is difficult for some people to function efficiently in a disorderly physical environment, and it is equally difficult for others to function well in a disorderly mental space. It is true for me that a peaceful environment nurtures a peaceful thought process, and yet I noticed that I can do all the outer arranging I want but if my mindset is one of disarray it remains difficult for me to have a satisfying experience with meditation.

A friend put it this way: "I get rid of the relationship, I change the job, I paint my house, all of them excellent ideas and they help immediately. After all is said and done, if inside I'm the same me, soon my life will reproduce the previous circumstances faithfully."

So I've learned to do some mind tidying as a way to provide a more hospitable space to do my meditation work. I ask the same useful questions I apply to a disorderly desk to my mind: "What is out of order in my inner life? What needs to be rearranged or prioritized inside?" And because I learned the power of beginning with one small thing, I do the same with my inner household. I move quietly and mindfully, satisfied with small moments of peace.

Helpful ideas in regard to creating inner orderliness have been:

To Persevere

Hang in there when doing inner work, I have to remind myself and others. So much in our culture is geared toward instant results, from microwaved food to instant rebates, that I find it slinks in and influences me to expect quick results in meditation. So if I sit still and meditate and nothing happens, I might be tempted to look elsewhere for better, quicker results. In practicing perseverance, I became fond of the phrase "Something is happening on the unseen side of life," which helped me remember that I can't always see the long view of the effects my meditation practice is having.

To Make Amends Quickly

I grew up Catholic and learned about the practice of formal confession when I was too young to really understand its power. Friends who grew up Catholic shared similar youthful misunderstandings of what the practice was and confessed that they would make up transgressions in the confessional because they didn't want to appear to be too good. As an adult I have learned how valuable it is to have a place of safety to share what I regret.

Instead of a formal confessional, I value the role that prayer partners have in my life and I count my years in formal therapy as one of the most valuable contributions to inner peace I have received. Being able to share your regrets in an openhearted manner is like cleaning a window of accumulated dust and grime and being able again to see clearly what is going on. I recommend finding a safe and trusted friend, or a professional, to share your heart's burdens as a powerful ingredient to finding inner peace. When it is possible to make amends (unless doing so would cause further harm) through apologizing to someone you may have wronged, it is advisable to do so as quickly as is practical so as to relinquish associated feelings of guilt and worry.

To Be Honest Kindly

An important step toward sobriety in the Alcoholics Anonymous 12-step program is to acknowledge what is actually going on, for without that recognition it is difficult to make strong progress toward recovery. Without an honest view of what is going on, all efforts and other steps tend to collapse on themselves.

Being honest with yourself is not an invitation to be cruel with yourself or others when and if you discover something disconcerting inside. It is rather an invitation to practice embracing with compassion what you discover. Criticism doesn't lead to kindness, only kindness creates more kindness, and where better to begin than with yourself.

A too fast pace and a too busy schedule make it difficult to accurately and kindly assess what is going on, and without that assessment, progress in meditation can be thwarted.

To Keep Spiritual or Inspiring Company

Take time to learn from people whom you admire by taking into your thought how they operate in the world so that you can consider if there is some way you can adopt the strength they exhibit. Christian friends are fond of saying to me when I ask them about a particularly difficult decision, "What would Jesus do?" I can find my own way to apply that idea by calling to mind someone, living or dead, whom I respect and ask myself, "What would _____ do in this situation?"

Keeping company with people whose values and life choices inspire you is likely to affect you, and keeping company with people who practice meditation or other spiritual practices is likely to nurture the idea that spiritual practice is normal. If you can't physically keep company with others who practice, you can do so through reading or joining social networks online where spiritual practice is a way of life.

When I first began to tidy up the company I kept, it was disconcerting to realize that some of the people I spent a lot of time with either did not value spiritual practice as a valid pursuit or good-naturedly tolerated my interest. In some cases I realized it would be best to spend less time with people who frustrated my practice simply because I was strongly influenced by their preferred use of time. In other cases I realized that I could continue to keep company with people who didn't share my spiritual interests or practices because, since I already knew their opinion, I refrained from disclosing to them my interest in spirituality or expecting them to participate in my enthusiasm.

To Listen Generously

I recently came across a beautiful phrase: "to listen generously." I believe it comes from Dr. Rachel Naomi Remen's training in which students are taught how to work with patients experiencing tremendous loss. In small groups, the students are given one instruction: listen generously.

To me that is even more beautiful than listening attentively. To listen generously evokes the image of dropping any desire to correct, teach, direct, hint, or advise. I can call to mind times when I have been listened to generously and the feeling of sanctuary that experience was. Tidying up the way I listened to the people around me was a way of training me to listen to myself and to the world of inspiration within me by generously giving my all to my meditation.

Listening generously is habit-forming because, once started, the effects and benefits of doing so begin to be progressively more rewarding and compelling, and eventually more enjoyable even than sharing a personal opinion.

To Speak Mindfully

There are many ways to tidy up the way you speak, from speaking less on impulse to speaking less altogether. Noticing your speech is another practice that fosters a mindset in which meditation flourishes. There are at least two ways to practice speaking mindfully.

First is the outer form when you're speaking to others. I try to keep this question in focus: "Is this the most beautiful way that I can say what I want to say?" Or I ask before committing to saying something, "What am I adding to the world's peace and harmony by saying this?"

Second is the inner form of mindful speaking when you are addressing yourself, either about other people or about yourself. I like to ask myself, "Is my mind a safe place for other people's reputations?" Or "Would you say what you just said about yourself to a child?"

Forest, Fields, and Flowers

In the mid-1980s, I rekindled my interest in spirituality and enrolled in a series of classes that had one thing in common: lots of guided meditation. I discovered quickly that meditation was important to living a spiritual life, and so I put myself to the task every time the teacher said, "Close your eyes, take a few deep breaths, and imagine you are in a forest . . ."

Whether it was a forest or a field of flowers, when I closed my eyes I saw nothing, just a play of light and darkness that resembled the screen of a TV not properly receiving a channel. And with that fuzzy vision came a sense of despair about my ability to "get it." Week after week I listened to the enthusiastic reports of fellow students who appeared to see in colorful detail every element of the guided meditations. I began to retreat into the feared thought that shortly I would be discovered as lacking the necessary spiritual awareness to meditate properly. Meditation exercises began to produce a state of agitation rather than turning my mind into an unwavering flame in a windless place. I felt irritable and unsuccessful.

Until, that is, another student in the class had the courage to speak up and say that he felt none of the sensations being described by classmates. He asked what he had been doing incorrectly and what could he do to improve. From that moment on, I breathed a little easier, having been reminded by his question that there is no one-size-fits-all solution for most things in life, including how to meditate. I began to meet other good-natured people who sincerely wanted to meditate and experience the power of the ancient practice, but who struggled with everything from sitting still, seeing or feeling expected images or sensations, stilling the mind, or maintaining enough interest for sustained practice.

A Mini-flash of Insight

My first helpful insight came when I read the instructions for how to meditate in chapter six of the Bhagavad Gita. I expected to find there step-by-step details, and I was surprised to read only a simple set of instructions basically guiding the students to sit up straight in a clean place, close their eyes, and keep thought one-focused:

> *Once seated, strive to still your thoughts.*
>
> Bhagavad Gita 6:12

It wasn't enough. I still did not know how to do it.

In my frustration, I decided that it was going to be up to me to find or design a practice of my own, and I might as well begin by doing what I enjoyed. I began to explore different ways to meditate and borrowed a little bit of everything I learned. Later, when I began teaching spiritual practices to others, this attitude became the key to encouraging students to develop their own practice of meditation: to discover how to do it their own way and with an explorer's attitude. I invited students to adopt an attitude of watchfulness, and to be open to where that led them.

I had begun in the same way, by simply sitting, just like it said in the Bhagavad Gita. I closed my eyes, and instead of trying to see something, or trying to think something or feel something, I started instead to notice what happened when I sat down in this way and observed. I approached the time of sitting with curiosity and a sense of discovery, deciding to let what wanted to happen, happen, neither trying to achieve something nor trying to quell my disappointment if nothing happened at all. I didn't know exactly what a quiet mind was supposed to be like—or more accurately, I had forgotten—I only knew I craved it.

Because I didn't know what I was reaching for, I took a step back and surrendered the idea of getting somewhere with meditation. What I couldn't know was that this was one of the keys that unlocks the door to a peaceful inner experience, with another being the willingness to sit still.

With less trying, and more gentle allowing, I came to see that my willingness to sit still at the same time, in the same place for short periods of time, was like an invitation to "whatever it is" to come to me. At least that is what it felt like. Like a cat that wants to sit on the lap of a restless person, whose quick movements make it impossible for the cat to settle down in its particular way, the quietness I craved had no way to come to me until I began to sit so as to make its presence welcome. Starting with external matters and progressing to thoughts and attitudes, I began to learn how to foster a welcoming frame of mind for peace to be witnessed.

First Important Steps

The Bhagavad Gita, in chapter 6, verses 11–12, instructs, "Select a clean spot, neither too high nor too low, and seat yourself firmly on a cloth, a deerskin, and kusha* grass. Then, once seated, strive to still your thoughts." I realized this passage describes two phases in the practice.

First, the words to me meant I was to select a spot, if possible, that belongs to the meditation practice alone (which I deal with more completely in chapter three). Prepare this spot, and yourself, as if preparing for a visit from someone you admire and whose company you respect. The

....

* Kusha grass is a tropical grass with an ancient history and mythological origins. Rather than attempt an explanation of the symbolism and meaning of a cloth, a deerskin, and kusha grass here, I take this direction to convey appropriate respect and mindfulness in preparing your place to meditate.

spot is described in the Bhagavad Gita as neither too high nor too low, which I came to understand is part of the Bhagavad Gita's overall invitation to moderation, and which has continued to serve as a reminder for me to be dedicated but not fanatical; to be enthusiastic without trying too hard. I came to repeat the phrase "neither too high nor too low" when preparing to sit, especially when I would come upon dry spells in meditation and the quiet-mind I was courting seemed to be even further out of reach than when I first started meditating (which I deal with in chapter eight).

I used the phrase to help coax myself back into the simplicity of being willing to sit, no matter what happened. "And seat yourself firmly on a cloth, a deerskin, and kusha grass," in its simplicity, proved to be immensely practical, that is, after I got over wondering what kusha grass is, where I was going to find it, and if a deerskin was truly necessary. In the end I took it all to be a symbol of preparing the place for meditation with respectful attention, whether I sat on a chair, a skin, or a cushion.

An ideal seat for meditation for me is something that is neither too soft nor too hard. Grain-filled cushions typically used in yoga studios are perfect for me. In the beginning, sitting without back support contributed to being able to stay awake for the exercise, whereas too comfort-able an environment could cause me to fall asleep.

Later I was able to practice my meditation anywhere and at any time—even in bed, first thing in the morning, because I looked forward to the time, which seemed more delicious than sleep. However, in the beginning, a reclined posture would sometimes lead me back to sleep. Even if sitting in too comfortable a chair, I found it easy to nod off. More helpful was to sit on the floor on a cushion suffi-ciently high to not cause discomfort in my knees, and then, once seated, according to the instructions, to go on to step two—to strive to still thinking.

For me, though, that next step didn't come for a while, several weeks in fact. I wasn't ready to start striving for anything. I was merely focused on establishing the routine of showing up at a certain time with a certain attitude, and that in itself was producing effects. I felt good about my effort and was happily more peaceful as a result. I certainly didn't think in those beginning weeks that I had any chance of successfully stilling my thoughts. I took some relief when I continued reading the Bhagavad Gita and discovered that one of the central characters, Prince Arjuna, had similar challenges and said, in what I imagined might have been a voice of frustration:

O Krishna, the stillness of divine union which you describe is beyond my comprehension. How can the mind, which is so restless, attain lasting peace? Krishna, the mind is restless, turbulent, powerful, violent; trying to control it is like trying to tame the wind.

Bhagavad Gita 6:33–34

So I didn't try to tame my mind; instead, I made friends with it. By that I mean I dropped my mental fight with what I discovered inside. I became a friendly observer of "inside," and in so doing, became aware of the layered nature of my inner world of thought: I could observe what was happening as if I were two separate people, one engaged in an event of sitting, and the other concerned only with watching what was happening. Later, I came to meet a third person (or point of view) inside, the one who was aware of both the observer and the actor. However, before I met any of these points of view within, I had to make a habit of sitting. I had to make a regular appointment to sit.

TRY THIS

First Attempt

Using something like a smartphone, a bedside clock, or a kitchen timer, set a device to let you know when ten minutes have passed. Before you start the countdown, turn off all other sound makers in your home—TV, music, cell phone, e-mail notifications—if possible.

Then begin. Sit.

Choose a comfortable place to sit that supports good posture. Too comfortable may lead to falling asleep. Try to have no expectation. To me that means letting whatever appears in your mind to come and go as it will. Adopt an attitude of watchfulness. At first, let your eyes look ahead of you and slightly down, and then gently allow the eyelids to close.

If the doorbell unexpectedly rings, or the neighbor fires up a chain saw in their backyard, try not to become agitated, but instead use these distractions as tools to strengthen your ability to focus or to notice what happens inside when you detect unwanted distractions.

After the ten minutes is complete, sit for a moment longer with your eyes open. Try not to rush or move too quickly into the next activity of your day.

Make a date with yourself to engage in this exercise every day at an appointed time for one week. You may notice that time seems to slow down or speed up during your meditation time, and you may become aware of changes in your body temperature, or you may even become aware of smells and sounds around you. You don't have to do anything with this information, just become aware of what you notice.

KEYS:

1. Surrender the idea of getting somewhere with meditation.

2. Be willing to practice sitting quietly every day.

The Sounds of Silence—Food for Thought

I once complained to a meditation teacher about insects being allowed free access into the meditation room and buzzing around my ears, causing intense agitation to rise up. The teacher responded to me by saying, "You're courting the presence of the divine but you're more interested in an insect." I remembered this when thinking of what my first yoga teacher taught me: that when we are fully engaged in the posture we are practicing, we ought to be able to do so on Main Street in rush-hour traffic without being disturbed. I remember these two guides with fondness whenever I'm becoming too serious about any part of practice. I also let myself get up and remove the insects if they appear and I also remember to get up if I find myself on Main Street, and relocate to a better place to practice, if possible—even though, if necessary, I'll practice anywhere. Silence, another meditator reminded me, is not the absence of sound or distractions from the world around you; it is more likely the absence of the ability for sounds and distractions to impinge upon your serenity. So silence contains everything, which is why, I believe, some people experience it as being intensely rich and full.

3

WORKING WITH A RESTLESS MIND

It is true that the mind is restless and difficult to control. But it can be conquered, Arjuna, through regular practice and detachment.

BHAGAVAD GITA 6:35

What Does It Mean if I Can't?

"It is true that the mind is restless and difficult to control," Krishna says to Prince Arjuna in the Bhagavad Gita, acknowledging in a beautiful, down-to-earth way the fluid and constantly moving nature of our minds, "but it can be conquered, Arjuna, through regular practice and detachment." I would abandon the words "control" and "conquer" and rewrite this instruction for today with different words. Typical of the Bhagavad Gita, however, if the reader focuses on the application of "regular practice" and "detachment," neither control nor conquering will be of any interest anyway. Be committed to your schedule but not to the outcome, is how I understand it.

Nevertheless, you may encounter times when it is difficult to stay with your practice. "If you can't practice, perhaps it means you ought not to for a while." I remember giving this counsel to a student who was going through both fear and grief because she hadn't been able to meditate for several weeks (which I discuss further in chapter four with pointers for what you may expect when you begin a regular practice). I remember the amazement on her face when I said the words to her that had helped me so much when I was stuck: "Nothing terrible will happen if you don't meditate." It had not occurred to her that it would be OK to stop for a while, or that it might be exactly the relief she needed: to take a break and let it pass. In time, she came back to her practice with less pressure to perform perfectly and more freedom to deviate from the schedule, and even to break free from it entirely from time to time. I encouraged her to create her own practice schedule and to make up her own curriculum for meditation practice. Again she was relieved because she had felt constricted by what she considered to be a "right way to do it" and hadn't imagined it could be possible to make it up from scratch for herself. We jokingly agreed to stop being concerned about imaginary meditation police on the lookout for protocol violators.

When students have difficulty with fluctuations in practice, I sometimes recommend a remedy that worked very well for me. I keep my appointment with meditation, but I let myself do anything I want during the allocated time: read a book, complete a Sudoku puzzle, anything. I just show up at the same time and the same place, if possible, because showing up there and then does something to sustain the momentum of my practice, even if I am not going to practice meditating for a while. Momentum is created by routine. "Same time, same place" is a formula for good results with meditating. There was a period of time when I meditated in a particular chair at a certain time. After a while, I could not look at the chair without thinking "meditate" and breathing a little deeper. After a longer while, it just didn't seem OK to sit in that chair to watch TV. I was beginning to build an attitude of devotional awareness associated with that chair. It made me think of a documentary I saw on the art of tea drinking that described how teapots and cups over centuries of use become more valuable because of the way regular use impacts them.

Expect the Unexpected

Studying and practicing meditation has been filled with unexpected learning and surprising benefits. In retrospect, some of the benefits seem reasonable to associate with meditation, but others were truly surprises and some were even unpleasant. I didn't expect—and frankly didn't enjoy—encountering disappointment, difficulties, and growing pains along the way of learning to sit in blissful peace.

Among the benefits that were pleasant is that the practice itself became easier and easier, most likely because of the regularity with which I practiced. That being the nature of practice: over time, with sustained and repeated engagement, things just get easier through rhythmic repetition and regularity. As I got into the routine of things, a sense of confidence and familiarity arose and I began to know what to expect from the practice. At least that is what I thought. The regular practice—it seemed—was laying down the foundation for something larger to rest on. Without the foundation of regular practice, the subtleties of silence couldn't be revealed. I also noticed with delight that I actually was becoming less and less attached to expectations of the practice. I was simply enjoying doing it. It was helpful to read the plainly stated acknowledgment in the Bhagavad Gita that the mind is truly difficult to control. It helped me calm down about the times when I didn't feel like meditating, or when I broke my routine, or couldn't get into the mood to be still. It helped me feel less like I was the only person in history who had a restless mind, and more forgiving about coming back gently to the practice when I was able. With this generosity toward my weaknesses, I encouraged myself to keep at it, and became better and better and better at keeping my appointment with sitting.

Among the unpleasant effects is that sometimes, without warning, without logical explanation, meditation would become impossibly hard to do. I would experience sitting in meditation to be like sitting in a major traffic jam: no movement and no escape. I would sometimes have the thought that I had been catapulted back to the very beginning of my practice, and it felt frustrating. I was grateful that my musician's background had equipped me to frame this within the filter of my music practice experience. There were days in which the instrument I loved to play, the very one that seemed to be like an extension of my hands, would feel awkward, like an alien object absent instructions. At such times, forcing through practice seemed to make things worse, whereas stepping away from the instrument for a while created the space I needed for matters to regain their balance.

Fixed Ideas

The student who was struggling with her practice was stressed because she was trying to conform to a previously learned idea of how to practice that was too strict and she couldn't let go of it. Rigid ideas about how to practice, or about anything for that matter, can get in the way of progress. Sometimes we begin studying something and even though we are new to the subject, we nevertheless may bring with us fixed ideas we picked up from others. Such fixed ideas may come from a teacher who has found a method that works, but who does not have the flexibility to adapt the method to students' needs. Sometimes the fixed ideas come from our culture and from the people who are our role models. When I was a young man, I somehow picked up the idea that meditation was something otherworldly, mystical, and possibly dangerous, and maybe for that reason, deeply interesting to me. These ideas were so strong in me that they got in the way of the normal and quite naturally nurturing experience that sitting still and being quiet produces. I was expecting something else. These expectations had to be set aside gently before I could make significant progress.

Once I discovered I had fixed ideas about meditation, it became easier to identify similarly fixed ideas about other practices, such as prayer for example—ideas that kept me stuck in the past and prevented me from establishing a prayer practice. I had to do the same letting go of old ideas about what prayer is that I did with meditation. Prayer, like meditation, I discovered—contrary to my early religious upbringing—exists in many diverse forms; there is no right way or wrong way to pray. It is a ludicrously impossible position to support that there is only one way to practice spirituality.

As I softened my opinion about what prayer is, I began to notice that I was attached to an idea that prayer had to be eloquent, filled with words of a near perfect poetic form. I had to let go of that, and when I did, I started to encounter prayer in a variety of forms, some of which crossed the boundary between meditation and prayer in that they were as much about the silences between words as they were about actual word-concepts; as much about movement as they were about being still. I got to liberate my childhood concept of prayer and entertain newer ideas. I accomplished this in part through sitting in meditation and examining my thoughts about prayer. I sat with questions such as "Does prayer require you to get on your knees?" "Whose attention am I attempting to get with prayer?" "What is prayer for?" "To whom is prayer addressed?" Soon after I began examining my concepts of prayer during meditation, I started to notice and appreciate all kinds of prayer, some with strict numbers of recitation, others with movements, some on knees and others not. If you choose one of these methods, that's just great, and you're not offtrack if you don't pray in a particular way. I know that now, and that confident knowing, I believe, came from meditating. Effective prayers are, in my opinion, the ones that are truly personal, so trust yourself because your honest attempt will lead you to an authentic experience.

The point is, whether you are learning how to pray or how to meditate, by abandoning fixed ideas about how it ought to be and adopting a simple attitude of exploration, you will be helping yourself toward satisfying progress. A fixed idea is one that is rigid and inflexible, and it affects everything around it because of its "stuckness." I imagine that you can call to mind an idea of your own that is pretty much fixed. An idea, for example, that no matter what anyone else tells you, and even if you know your idea isn't fully supportable, you will stay true to it, through thick or through thin; you won't budge, even if you know budging might be the appropriate next step. Perhaps there are times in life when such solidness is called for. I propose that a more flexible approach is better suited to making progress in learning about meditation. Krishna's advice on conquering the mind is to apply these two things: regular practice and detachment. His instructions about the practicalities may be vague but the directions for the mental approach are specific and point to an attitude of willingness and regularity. I take this to mean practice regularly and be flexible.

This Shouldn't Be Happening to Me

One of the recurring stumbling blocks facing students of spirituality is that of feeling unworthy when challenges emerge along the way. It can pop up when a student feels ashamed because of a situation in which they discover themselves, one that does not match their idea of what a student of spirituality should be experiencing. Whether that is a block in practice, or a relationship that is dissolving emotionally, or they lose their job, they may become distracted or embarrassed because of what is happening.

They may have a fixed idea that because now that they are on a spiritual path, those sorts of things shouldn't happen to them. Sometimes this leads the student to resist asking for help because they feel unworthy of support; they may even resist taking advantage of the available support systems, such as contacting friends, prayer partners if they have one, or mentors. It can be very difficult to reach a person who has gone down that path, because they may isolate or mask what is happening by behaving normally. They may be conflicted by understanding that their self-critical thoughts are unwarranted and at the same time by having contradictory thoughts such as "I'm a failure." Such self-defeating ideas belong in the category of thoughts that go something like this: "If you are spiritual, you will never have poor health or any challenges of any kind, and if you do, there is something essentially, spiritually speaking, wrong with you." Even though this idea doesn't match reality, and even though everyone around a person in whom such an idea has become lodged will tell them it isn't so, some continue to believe their private thoughts while nodding their head in agreement to what is being said.

Here is a more reasonable description of life, spiritual or otherwise, that I think is important to keep in mind right from the beginning of setting up a meditation practice: Everybody makes mistakes as part of the process called living, and in that process are unexpected challenges, ups, downs, and in-betweens. It is all part of the ordinary complex process of being alive, and no one is exempt from it. As the title of Jim Rosemergy's book explains, *Even Mystics Have Bills to Pay.* If a person has a fixed idea about what spiritual living looks like, especially if it is an idealized version of perfection, then the ordinary twists and turns of life can be confusing to them, and they may even become embarrassed when they, as they most certainly will, find themselves in one of those moments. And so it is that they turn away from their practice, whether that is prayer or meditation, or they shrink from taking refuge in their spiritual community at the very times when those activities might be the most helpful. The way out and through is not to retreat, and neither is it to conquer through combat. The way out is characterized by generosity of spirit and kindness toward yourself.

Sitting in quietness without a fixed agenda is a way of encouraging ourselves to take in the imperfections of life with a little more gentleness, less embarrassment, shame, or self-criticism. Even if you notice that during your sitting practice you don't seem to be able to adopt a positive frame of mind, and worry continues to find its way into your thought, you may start to realize that you are going through something that everyone goes through. The fact is, sometimes worry is intensely present. With this generous approach, you may begin to develop an understanding of such things as appropriate fear, appropriate concern and/or grief without slipping into the kind of denial practice that turns away from, or sugarcoats, uncomfortable feelings and experiences. There is no amount of worrying you can do that will change reality. There is no amount of emphatic positive thinking you can do that will cover what you really think. Your inner life will change dramatically, however, when you let your thought land without force, authentically and gently, on an affirmative concept that it accepts without resistance. When that happens, it appears to affect the view of everything outside yourself.

When I began to practice meditation regularly, I discovered to my relief that I could have two opposing beliefs at the same time and it didn't mean I was lacking in spirituality or that I needed to be repaired. Through gentle observing, I noticed I could have both faith and fear simultaneously, and it wasn't my task to deny or affirm either one. Instead, I learned to gently uncover each thought that passed through my mind and watch it compassionately. That became my work, and that did wonders to ground me in a peaceful, accepting frame of mind. Ultimately, that gentle work equipped me to face and navigate through some of the truly difficult challenges and disappointments in my life.

Familiarity Breeds Contentment

Once I learned how to compensate for not being able to *see* in my mind's eye what I was being asked to imagine, I was able to experience guided meditation in a new way. I learned to listen to what was being told in the meditation instructions as if listening to a story being recited. It doesn't matter whether or not I can visually see what a friend is telling me when recounting their recent experience with something, I just have to listen to the story and enjoy it. In a similar way, I learned when listening to a guided meditation that I could enjoy the directions as if they were the recitation of a story told to me by a friend. Some of my friends whom I love dearly take too long to tell a story for my taste, but I love them so much that I cherish the storytelling anyway. I practice the same approach when following guided meditation: "Why not enjoy it like a story?" I could understand what was being said, and that turned out to be enough.

This change in perception about what using my imagination could be like allowed me to open up to a suggestion, made by a teacher, to create an imagined inner space to which I could mentally return for quiet and meditative introspection. The childlike simplicity of the imaginative venture appealed to me immensely. I was to create a space inside my own mind accessible only to me through the story I told myself. I didn't have to see the images of the place I was creating; I just had to describe it to myself as if in a conversation. I decided that an elevator down into the earth, with a complex security code entered on a numeric pad, would do the trick to create an atmosphere of security. The descent to the underground lair in my thoughts became an enjoyable mind-adventure. Surprisingly, I derived a lot of pleasure from visiting my inner world and found that the ritual of the mental journey to it produced a peaceful state of mind in which I could be single-minded, present, and peaceful.

Down in the earth, in the lair of my imagination, I had a place now where there was sanctuary, a place I would visit frequently to rest and regroup. Sometimes I imagined there was a kind of oracle there to consult with about a question on my mind, and other times I imagined having a phone conversation with someone I admire. Part of the success of this particular method is that I had to walk myself through an elaborate system of entering the access code, descending in the elevator, and refreshing my description of what was waiting there. Later I began to see the connection between repeated actions and how they can set up a rhythm that contributes to a meditative state. The growing familiarity of the imagined inner place developed into a deep sense of contentment and ease. After a while I realized that I didn't need to tell myself the story or imagine the space inside to enter the state of contentment; I had become so familiar with it that the practice could give way to simple, straightforward sitting in silence.

Familiarity can cause a sense of contentment and confidence, and perhaps, I'm learning, the serenity of contentment is necessary to open the doorway to what is not yet known. There could be some apprehension about opening unknown states of mind, and without the comfort of familiar practices and experiences one may shy away from going deeper. In a way, familiarity through repetition has provided me the comfort to become aware of things that I had not noticed before. This has been as true in meditation as it has been in other activities where I have repeated the same actions faithfully, such as in my twice-weekly run around the local lake. For years I have taken nearly the same path, with minor variations, around a scenic lake in the neighborhood, and through the years I have started to know the area very well.

I know the location of fallen oak trees and the mosses that grow on them, the places where wildlife are likely to be encountered, and places where the path is more strenuous than others. These details of the journey have been integrated into the whole experience, and although I remain aware of them, I now have them catalogued and remembered so that they compete less and less for my attention. Instead, I find my available attention has been freed up to look at the places between locations of familiarity for what else might be there that I hadn't noticed before. I find myself looking for spiderwebs reflecting the light, delighted at how many there are that I hadn't seen before; or looking into the dark spots where my eyes hadn't loitered before and noticing the textures and colors that had always been present but unnoticed. I experience this as an awakening of awareness, and the result is a lusher experience of my time at the lake.

Some of the Silence Stays with You

It may be easier to describe what the process of awakening to your inner life *is not* like than it is to describe what it *is* like. It's not like a movie that you go to see fully knowing how the plot works out, or a movie in which you can predict just how much you will enjoy it because every movie you've ever seen has been very much like it. Typically, when the doorway to your inner life cracks open, what's on the other side can be unexpected and unlike any movie you've ever seen before. It reveals something that is captivating and possibly surprising because, until that moment of awakening, it has not been in your awareness. The experience of awakening to your inner life is more like reading a book that leaves you thinking about some aspect in it for weeks after, or like the days after seeing a movie that has an ending you weren't quite expecting and maybe don't even understand fully yet, or a twist in the plot gives you ample occasion to wonder how it applies to your own life. Practicing meditation may well cause you to wonder about things, question what you think, and reconsider what you believe to be true, not only in those moments set aside for sitting, but at unexpected moments in your life.

In 2007, I visited an ashram in Varanasi, India. Every morning, I joined the teenage boys at six a.m. for yoga. They had been meditating already but I needed those few extra minutes to get my spot in the shared shower and wake up. I joined them just as they started to chant three aums.* I've chanted in America before, but on the second floor of an ashram staring at the sacred river Ganges, with the oranged sun climbing through the pollution haze, is not a scene I've played in anywhere before, not even close. One boy was late and missed the initial pre-yoga chanting. At the end of the practice, he sat quietly while everyone left. After a long deep breath, he sang a long extended "aum," and the world stopped. I didn't expect it and it expanded my idea of what chanting aum could be like. Those remaining in the room either left quietly or sat and waited for him to complete his practice. I had never heard such an aum by one person. At first I thought it was a trick of acoustics, an echo perhaps. Then I thought it was some special training like those multi-noted Tibetan throaty chants. No. It was just a young boy immersed in his god-idea, and from him came this note that had other sounds woven into it. It was high and low at the same time. Buzzing and resonating smoothly at once, it filled all time and space and packed the room with holiness, and the world stopped.

And when the aum stopped, the world stayed stopped.

....

* "Aum," or "om," is a word used in various faith traditions, particularly Hinduism, as an incantation at the beginning and end of sacred readings or prayer practice. The Mandukya Upanishad explains the meaning of each syllable, which in brief, symbolize the beginning, continuation, and dissolution of creation, and are associated respectively with the gods Brahma, Vishnu, and Shiva. As sacred syllable, "aum" represents the impersonal Absolute Source of all that is, which in itself is considered to be unknowable. Therefore, a symbol is necessary to represent it: ॐ

There was none of that "Oh, you sing so well" or "I just love how you aum" or "Your aum really touched me." Just agreement in the air and watchful silence. Though a part of the world stayed stopped, the activities and sounds of its life-blood went on and on and crept in over the walls of the ashram, into the windows and over the floors. Life—loud, fast, busy, hard, big—continued to be present and approaching. Yet a little bit of his aum lingered with me the whole day, like a book or poem that stays with me long after I'm done with it, one that awakened me to something that I hadn't seen or heard before; that opened a door I don't think can ever be closed again. Had I hurried out of the classroom to satisfy the significant hungry grumbling in my belly, I might have missed it. The experience wasn't part of the predicted curriculum of yoga asanas, it happened in the crack between scheduled events.

Although I cannot predict it, or force it to happen, it is sometimes the case that when I rise from sitting in meditation, some of the silence I meet in the practice lingers with me for the whole day, and sometimes even beyond a day.

TRY THIS

Intentional Space

Create an intentional meditation space in your home, if possible. It can be a whole room or a corner of a room. It can be a small table or a shelf on a book stand. Ideally, try to use this space for no other purposes for the next seven days. Only meditate there. Consider creating a focus point in your space, like an altar. You could use a small table or surface for this purpose and place items of significance to you on it. Use items that inspire and uplift you. These could include photos of children or mentors, or items that carry great meaning for you. You could also add items that are simply beautiful to you.

Take a moment, for the next seven days, just before your scheduled practice of sitting, to review the items on your display, reminding yourself silently why you chose them. This review process directly before your practice of sitting can become a ceremony that in itself, when repeated faithfully, can help establish in you the mindset of meditation. Consider it to be as important a part of your practice as the sitting itself.

You could elaborate on the ceremony by adding elements to it, such as lighting a candle. For example, each time you sit, light a candle in memory of someone, either living or not, who has made a beneficial impact on your life. While lighting the candle, think of the ways in which their influence has contributed to your life. Take a moment to sit with the thoughts, perhaps observing the flame while you do so.

And Now I Lay Me Down to Rest

Creating a meditation routine can be challenging for some people if their daily schedule changes a lot, or if they travel for work, or if they are raising a family. In such cases, I recommend using bedtime as an appointment for some type of meditative exercise. At some point, you're going to have to go to bed, and when you do, you can use the opportunity to begin a regular practice of some technique that is easy enough to perform, even if you are tired after a long day. One such technique is to begin a review of the day in reverse with eyes closed. Begin by thinking about the very last person you had any engagement with, whether in person or a conversation on the phone or through an e-mail. To the best of your ability, bring that person into your awareness. If you can imagine their face, do so, or you may simply think about them. Try not to replay the content of the conversation or communication, and instead think of the person, their name or their face. Then state silently to yourself, "[Name], I bless you, I set you free from all expectations, and give thanks for your life." After an unhurried moment, think back to the next person and repeat the exercise. Going back through the people of your day in this way may indeed induce sleep more quickly than you expected, which is fine and is a beautiful way to go to sleep. If you didn't have any conversations or communications with anyone on a particular day, you can do the exercise with people in your circle of friends and in your family, or you can do it with public figures.

Graces

Another repeating event in all people's lives is eating, so I recommend using it to introduce a practice of introspection or mindfulness. Eventually, these small practices create openness to a more substantial practice, and on their own have a significant effect on peace of mind. Whenever you are about to begin eating, I recommend taking a brief moment to be still. If you are concerned about drawing attention to the process while in public, you don't have to close your eyes. You don't have to do anything more than be still for a moment. In fact, taking a moment to be still and look at your food will contribute to your mindfulness. Silently notice the colors, the textures, the aroma before eating. The tradition of reciting a prayer, silently or out loud, before eating is referred to as "saying grace" and may be thought of as an expression of appreciation for the food about to be consumed. I like to take a moment before eating to imagine everything and everyone that was involved in making it possible for the meal to be in front of me. This practice helps me stay in contact with the world and helps prevent taking things and people for granted.

Slowing Down

Go to bed an hour earlier than usual for a week, and don't do anything stimulating or entertaining in that hour. Also, start your day an hour earlier for a week, and don't do anything stimulating or entertaining during that hour.

Give yourself time in the morning to set the tone for your day by moving about slowly and mindfully.

Practice arriving early for appointments, dates, and at destinations so that you can sit quietly for a while before getting into the flow of the activity.

KEYS:

1. Schedule meditation on your calendar, and keep the appointment even if you don't feel like meditating.

2. Create a space for your meditation practice, one that generates an atmosphere conducive to stillness and relaxation.

Food for Thought—What's the Hurry?

Every year at the organization where I work, the staff makes a conscious decision to declutter our schedule of events, classes, and activities. Each year, we are successful at doing so. Each year, we notice with grins, and sometimes a grimace, that the former busyness creeps back like the clamor of the city of Varanasi climbed back into the yoga classroom. Typically, a speeding up of our pace gradually sidles back in with more things to do and with fewer minutes to do them in; the moment of our purposeful decompression becomes a faded memory. We recalibrate annually because we notice that when we are rushing, we don't have time to be present for what is happening in the cracks between scheduled events, and as a result we sometimes overlook some of what makes life beautiful. I read that impatience is just another word for being in a hurry. Impatience is connected to moving fast—in my opinion, too fast. When I'm moving too fast, my available resources are invested in moving at that fast pace; and in the hurry, I rush over opportunities to notice, connect, and see the world around me. It is very difficult to experience connected, openhearted, compassionate communication when in a hurry.

When I am rushing through my life, consumed with everything I have to attend to, it becomes more and more likely that I will miss what is available to me. I notice that when I move through the world at this pace, I tend to do what a friend calls "wearing my grumpy pants." Poignantly, life is such that grumpiness makes it less likely that I will get more done, because grumpiness has the influence of alienating and repelling people. Worse, grumpiness has the effect of causing matters to take longer than they would ordinarily because of the friction it causes. It's difficult to practice being mindful and experience grumpiness at the same time. Mindfulness generates a slower speed and is, I think, an antidote to grumpiness.

It's easy to understand the value of moving through life at a mindfully slower pace, but the reality of contemporary life is that there is consistent insistence that everything hurry up and keep moving. There is a tremendous value placed on getting ahead, and to do that, one has to move faster and be on top of everything. Going faster can and does get you to your destination more quickly than going slower. It also reduces maneuverability, in the same way that turning and stopping effectively can be difficult and restricted in a too fast moving car.

If the pace of your life cannot be slowed down or decluttered right away, you can apply the remedy of slowing down your mind. You may even discover that the speeded-up pace of life comes more from the speed of your mind than it does from people and circumstances around you. A significant hindrance to slowing down is the cultural stigma that to be slow is to be lazy, or possibly not too bright. It is also associated with a "couldn't care less" attitude and may have to be reframed to appreciate the value of going slow without sacrificing creativity and responsibility. The point of slowing down the mind is not to zone out and disconnect from society; rather it could be seen as adopting the appropriate speed in which deep relationships can flourish naturally and productivity can grow out of mindful engagement. Slowing down attention can be reframed from a type of escape to being a way to discover and enjoy what is in each moment in places where before we rushed by. Eknath Easwaran, in *Take Your Time*, writes:

> *When your mind is still, you can work hard and be active every day of your life and still be at rest, because you will not be working under the goad of personal ambition. That's the secret of Gandhi, who worked for a selfless cause fifteen hours a*

day seven days a week even in his seventies but
never got exhausted, because, he said, "I am always
at rest."*

Slowing the mind is another one of those things that cannot be experienced by reading about it. It has to be given a chance to prove itself. It is the sort of thing that can be experienced as accumulative, starting off as something pleasant and progressing to being a well-known inner sanctuary to be referred to, even to retreat to. What I find encouraging is that anyone can practice slowing their mind because it requires no particular education or talent to do the basic practice. Rather than trying to still my mind, I prefer to practice slowing down my mind. I sometime use the phrase "I'm practicing being forgetful" to lightheartedly describe the sensation I sometimes have when sitting. Most likely you have had a moment like that, of being completely self-forgetful, a moment in which you forget yourself, or the movement of time seems to slow down. These moments can happen spontaneously when we are deeply engaged in something we are doing, wrapped up in the details. Usually, in moments like these I am typically very, very happy. Although "happy" isn't the most accurate

....

* Eknath Easwaran, *Take Your Time: How to Find Patience, Peace & Meaning* (Tomales, CA: Nilgiri Press, 1997), p.187.

word to describe the sensation; maybe "satisfied" is better, or perhaps "peaceful." The sensation is as if some part of me has come to a temporary stop while everything else is continuing. I think it may be what the Zen Buddhist phrase "No Mind" refers to, or what Eknath Easwaran calls a "still mind."

In *Take Your Time*, there is a helpful metaphor for framing the slowed-down, self-forgetful state I'm describing. Think of driving a car and imagine that your body is the vehicle, your mind is the engine, and you are the driver. Imagine that you know how to slow down the vehicle and park it when necessary, turn off the engine, and store the key safely in your pocket. Instead of doing all that, sometimes people leave their mind idling on the street with the key still in the ignition, gas being wasted, air being polluted, and the ominous possibility of an ill-intentioned, opportunistic thought to take the controls and drive the vehicle off. Perhaps you know what it is like to have your mind stolen by your thoughts? I remember the time when my car was stolen from an airport parking lot. I felt so helpless and frustrated, as well as disoriented. That is the same feeling I encounter when my life gets commandeered by fast-paced thinking. Someone else is driving my life around, and possibly at a reckless pace, taking me to activities that are not advisable for me to participate in, considering my state. There is no time to slow that driving-thought and examine it for accuracy and legitimacy, and no time to decide whether or not driving should be entrusted to it.

I think of turning off the engine and parking the car safely for a moment as what it means to have a still, quiet space in my life. When I used to be a volunteer for a pastoral care visitation organization catering to people with life-threatening diseases, I knew in advance that sometimes I would be visiting people who were in extremely distressing situations and that my visit could be emotional for me and possibly I would encounter visually disturbing scenarios of people looking gaunt and unwell. I developed the habit of arriving for my visitation appointment early enough to park the car safely outside, turn the engine off, and sit still in my car with my eyes closed for up to fifteen minutes. What I loved about the practice is that the quiet car was like a cocoon insulating me from the noise and bustle of the world, and yet not removing me entirely from it. I could still hear the world's activity, but it had been reduced in loudness and closeness enough so that I could sit and be still.

This practice turned out to make all the difference to me in a field of pastoral visitation in which people burn out quickly because of the emotional toll it can take. In those fifteen minutes, my mind slowed down and I sorted out what type of thinking should be driving me as I walked in to visit my client. The time in "mental park" helped my face and shoulders to relax; and more and more, the people I visited would report to me that an atmosphere of calm entered the room with me when I visited them. Had I come in with all my thoughts and fears, questions and concerns in driving position, I think a different atmosphere would have accompanied me into the room.

Turning off the engine and waiting for a while in a parked car to me is what it means to have a still, quiet time in your life on a regular basis where silence is available. It is a time in which you don't need to be attending to anything other than sitting, a time in which you have no duties to attend to, nothing to watch or care for outside of what you are doing in that silence. It may only last a few moments, and truly I think that with practice it can be achieved in a twinkling of an eye, because once you start nurturing yourself with this kind of silence—which I think of as nourishments or medicine for the harried soul—you'll realize how magnificent it is, you'll want more of it, and you'll be able to go further, longer with less of it, if necessitated by a sudden emergency of an emotional or trying situation.

Again, the practice of sitting still doesn't require retreating from the world, and being adept at the practice doesn't mean that no more unpleasant situations will take place in your life or around you. Not at all. Life has an interesting way of churning things up endlessly. When you have become comfortable taking time in silence, and you retreat to it with regularity, your quiet-mind will become a safe harbor when stressful things do happen. Your first response will be less frequently to become agitated because you will have practiced slowing and will have developed confidence in how slow, measured thoughts can help you meet the events of life.

4

WHAT HAPPENS NEXT?

The wise see that there is action in the midst of inaction and inaction in the midst of action. Their consciousness is unified, and every act is done with complete awareness.

BHAGAVAD GITA 4:18

You Can't Get There Through Talking About It

If the only thing you do as a result of reading this book is to begin an exploratory practice of sitting still for short periods of time on a daily basis, you will have fulfilled my dream of making a contribution to the peace in this world. I have so much trust and confidence in the cumulative effect of simply sitting still (on a consistent and sustained basis) that I completely expect the practice to produce beneficial awareness in you.

You can only experience it by doing it, not just talking about it. Here's an example to illustrate my point. A long time ago, I was teaching a class about the benefits of regular, structured, conscious giving—that is, the practice of charitable giving with a scheduled rhythm (because I believe rhythm builds momentum), without any attachment (free from manipulation or superstition) for the purpose of practicing generosity.

I felt confident that any person accepting my challenge to begin a practice of contributing money on a regular basis to an organization with which they felt some affinity and trust would after one year be able to look back and see a shift in their relationship to giving.

So assured was I about this practice that I offered a money-back guarantee to those people who would accept the challenge to make a one-dollar weekly contribution to the organization I served. After twelve months, I told them, if they did not experience a beneficial shift in awareness about giving and their connection to the community, they would be able to receive their fifty-two dollars back, no questions asked.

Many took me up on the challenge, and I think in all

the years I have presented this challenge, only one person ever petitioned to have their money back. As promised, I didn't ask for the reason. More important, among those who took on the practice of regularly contributing, several reported that it was exactly what they needed to take a step out of their comfort zone into a world of freedom around giving and receiving. Some developed into being among the strongest givers in their own spiritual communities and attributed their surge in creativity, freedom, and feelings of being connected to their practice of regular giving.

Most important, some reported that if they were to look back from this moment in which they were practicing givers and deliver an enthusiastic, passionate testimony to themselves, their selves in the past would likely not trust the statements completely because they had no reference in experience on which to base the trust. Now that they had completed the journey, one they had to start slowly, building their own momentum and developing their own confidence through testing the practice, they were aware of something that only experience can impart.

You can't get to that experience through talking about giving. You have to actually get involved. Your hands have to be in your pocket for it to become meaningful.

And so it is with meditation.

You can read about it and become an informed and knowledgeable student of styles and methods of schools of meditation, but you can't get to the land it points to any other way than to make the journey called "doing it," regularly, consciously, and with structure. And I suspect that nobody can accurately predict what exactly your own journey and discovery will be through meditation.

What May Be Expected

Peace and Quiet

One of the signs that your meditation practice is being effective is likely to be the reduction in the general amount of restlessness in you. Without losing interest in life and without losing your inclination to be creative and engaged in life, you may nevertheless experience what I call a reduction in "reaching." It is as if before the practice you may have had a sensation of something missing in life, a feeling that may have been the impetus for your search for a meaningful spiritual practice. After you began practicing, the compelling drive to fill that missing space may very well have subsided to give way to healthy curiosity about silence and a growing appreciation for your life as it is.

There is some relief in this awareness of your "enoughness" and the accompanying sense of being part of a larger scene that is being played out without any effort on your behalf. Although on one hand you may realize that the fact of your life is effortless, on the other hand you see also how inextricably interlinked your actions are with everyone and everything. You may notice that you begin to take your role and responsibility in life quite seriously and you develop the capacity to make important decisions and complete important tasks with clarity rather than urgency.

Shifts in Perception

Some people experience a change in perception of the world around them after beginning a regular meditation practice. For some, it comes as something pleasant, perhaps nothing more than a calming change in pace. Others experience a radical shift in everything, and their view of themselves and life around them changes substantially. Should this be the case, it becomes important to have routines and structures to lean on if during times like these you feel disoriented.

In other words, regular social engagement, working out at a gym on a regular schedule, participating in a reading club, and other structured activities contribute ease to what meditation practice may open up in your awareness. It is also helpful to have adequate sleep, good nutrition, and physical exercise to help nurture a sense of well-being. Time spent in nature can also have the effect of alleviating the kind of disorientation that may come when consciousness awakens to reality. Stepping back from practice or discussing developments with a mentor is invaluable.

You May Need a Break

It is worth mentioning that even advanced students of meditation may go through dry spells in which they cannot remember what it was like to feel the grounded connection they achieved at the start of their practice. This can be disturbing because, while that person will have a solid memory of the peace and quiet they experienced, at the same time feelings of frustration arise because they seem not to be able to reattain that state.

The best advice I received at such a time came as a surprise. I was advised to take a break from all practice of every kind. I was shocked and felt lost. So much of my identity and routine had become wrapped up in my meditation practice that without it I thought I would be rudderless. This advice also helped dislodge a hidden belief that was governing me: If I stopped practicing, something terrible would happen.

What I discovered was just the opposite in fact; the pause was exactly what I needed for something beneficial to take place. I took thirty days off and rediscovered natural balance. I rediscovered how much beauty life was full of and how many opportunities existed for mindfulness in everyday activity. I had become bogged down in practice rules and started to experience practice as something arduous that was separating me from life.

The pause in my routines helped me stop reaching, and I found that the peaceful, calm witness of my quiet-mind continued to be present and available, whether I was sitting in meditation, or shopping for groceries, or doing whatever was before me to do. I just needed a break from the formal practice to reset my perspective and remember to live.

Detachment

Practicing meditation may well result in the reduction of attachments. Attachment in this sense means that if you don't have it—whatever "it" is—you're not going to be happy, and because you don't have it, you'll be thinking about it a whole lot, and probably assessing yourself unfavorably for not having it. It can also mean that when you *do* have it, you will adjust your life, schedule, spending, and values to keep it. There are all kinds of ideas and events that fit what "it" might be. It could be a relationship, a job, an experience, or just about anything.

This kind of focus on something external displaces the awareness of inner peace with a promise to provide as much joy as your spiritual practice. Whereas people, positions, possessions, and events can and ought to bring tremendous joy and fulfillment, it is the case for each that they are temporal and have a limited shelf life in terms of their ability to satisfy us.

It is not a new idea that attachment and suffering are connected to each other, but nevertheless an idea that I need to keep fresh before me. I forget it when I get wrapped up in wanting to own something more desperately than is reasonable, or control an outcome, or influence a person. When I can detect an "if . . . then" dialogue in myself, I know I have some work to do regarding my attachments and priorities: "If I don't get this_____, then I'll be _____." Clinging to fixed projected outcomes is a way of narrowing focus and potentially obscuring alternative outcomes.

We put ourselves through a tremendous amount of stress because of the manner in which we want things. It isn't that things are bad to possess, it's the *way* of wanting them that is the issue. It is the attitude with which we want them. It isn't that we want a thing, it's how we want it that makes the difference between inner peace and inner pain. In the same way that closing your eyes with awareness for meditation is a completely different experience from shutting your eyes without awareness, it's the style or atmosphere of our wanting that causes the pain or the freedom. If the wanting is hot and fast moving, it is different from *welcoming*, which is spacious, cool, and flexible.

Spiritual teacher Ernest Holmes wrote:

> *What would be your reaction and mine if we knew the only thing we could take with us when we leave this world would be that which we really are? Would not our reaction be more kind and gentle? Would not our very possessions seem of less value?** *

At the heart of this idea is a question: How do we measure the worth of or the success and happiness of our lives? If it is by how many things we possess, or that we possess the correct things, or by how much attention we receive as a result of possessing something, or by how favorably we compare physically, in talents or ability to others, then I can see the potential for suffering.

....

* Jesse Jennings, ed., *The Essential Ernest Holmes* (New York: Jeremy P. Tarcher, 2002), pp. 185–86.

Understanding the difference between detaching and becoming uncaring is important. We can learn how to detach from painful ways of wanting without becoming disheartened or wishy-washy. There are important issues facing our world today, and becoming disconnected from them, or becoming unresponsive to our role in alleviating the suffering of others, is not what detachment is about. Gandhi suggested that the answer lies in where our focus is. Rather than being focused on, and attached to, a particular outcome, he suggests that we concentrate on our motive and also on our best endeavor:

> By detachment I mean you must not worry whether the desired result follows from your action or not, so long as your motive is pure, your means correct. Really, it means that things will come right in the end if you take care of the means and leave the rest to Him.*

Being attached to an outcome requires a lot of mental, emotional, and physical investment, particularly if things are not going the way I intend and I appear to be attached

....

* *Harijan* newspaper (April 7, 1946), as quoted in *Gandhi for the 21st Century: The Teachings of the Gita*, third edition, Anand T. Hingorani, ed. (Bhavan's Book University, 1998), p. 50.

to how things ought to work out. The first step in undoing attachment is to notice that it is happening, which you may detect through telltale signs like tenseness in the upper body—for example, in the chest or shoulders—or in a too tight clench of the lips or jaw, or in an uneasy feeling in your gut.

Feelings of stress, indignation, and self-righteousness are reliable gauges that frustration due to attachment is arising. If I can spot this happening, and I can sit down somewhere for a moment, I take a mental inventory of where else tension has crept in, and take in and exhale ten deep breaths. While I am doing that, I repeat to myself silently, "I am shifting my focus from the outcome, I'm focusing instead on who I am in this moment. I care about being authentic, mindful, and present."

Even if I can't find somewhere quiet to sit and breathe, I can typically perform the exercise anywhere, using these words or words similar. I don't always experience a miraculous shift in awareness, but I find the willingness to pause flavors every next action with a slowed-down pace in which clarity comes more easily.

It is easy for any number of compelling things I'm engaged in during the ordinary course of my life to seize control of my inner well-being. I can, for example, find myself deeply focused on worrying about the outcome of something, or feeling concerned about making a poor decision, or something similar. I may notice in such cases that I can zero in on my thought-attachment with unwarranted vigor and excessive energy. In these moments, I experience myself being, as my grandmother would put it, "not in my right mind."

I saw a bumper sticker that asked, "Have you ever stopped to think, and then forgot to start again?" I have. I have stepped out of being present for life because I began to obsess about something I had unsuspectingly become attached to, and forgot to step out of the obsession and back into life for quite a while. Now I see the wisdom in remembering to stop thinking in the future tense, and instead return my thought to observing what it is I am engaged in at the present time. In this regard, meditation has proven to be a valuable method of detaching from troubling thoughts.

Detachment means to me stepping away from destructive mental attitudes and is not the same as becoming apathetic or actionless. It is instead adopting an empowered type of action that I call *aware action*, or *awake action* or *restful alertness*. When unaware or asleep, I easily go the way of the crowd and forget to stand up and say something, like Jesus did to the mob gathering to stone a woman to death, and find myself instead being a complicit observer in the mob.

Detachment also does not mean being indifferent to the outcome, it does not mean being uncaring whether or not the woman is stoned to death. Nor does it mean working in this world without clear ideas, a plan, or strategy. It *does* mean that even though I "go for it" wholeheartedly, using my creative intelligence and committing fully to what I am doing, I introduce in my mind some spaciousness for the unknown and some flexibility in responding to the un-scheduled and unexpected. It *does* mean that even while I act, there is restful peace within me, and in my rest-ful peace I still get to believe in my work, I still get to be responsible for selecting actions that support my values while at the same time I create some space for the new and unexpected.

Attentive people who cultivate quiet-mind through meditation don't necessarily become complacent and with-drawn from the world. Their detachment from outcomes need not reduce them to bland, uncaring people who have no motives and no ambition. My experience is that cultiva-tion of a quiet-mind through meditating leads instead to reducing barriers between me and my world, increasing compassionate engagement and clarity about what is mine to do in this world. Since beginning to practice meditation, I have found it increasingly difficult to shirk responsibilities, or to avoid taking a stand in the face of injustice, or to hide from the suffering of others.

Clarity

Practicing meditation helped me become clearer on what meditation is and what it is not. Experimenting with different ways to meditate helped me become sensitive to differences in various mental states that arise while doing different things. I began to discover the dissimilarity between quietness of mind and busyness of mind. Each seemed to have its own temperature so to speak, or a unique pace and temperament. I started to notice the damaging aftereffects of allowing unsupervised reactivity as compared to the life-improving effect of more thoughtful responses during everyday communication. Fast, chaotic thinking I began to describe as warm or even hot thinking, whereas a mindful moment of contemplation felt spacious, flexible, and cool. Somehow, because I had familiarized myself with these differences, I seemed to develop the ability of moving from one type of mindset to another with growing ease, simply because I knew better what the destination felt like.

Now I notice that there are moments when I might be

powerfully engaged in something, such as a difficult conversation or a fast-moving negotiation, and if I realize my thought is too hot or the speed inside too dangerous, in that moment I notice it something internal will shift and events will slow down, at least internally from my perspective as I move into a calmer, cooler realm. I attribute this development to my meditative practices of sitting, journaling, and watching thought or breathing and so on. It seems I'll shift perspective, like a director in a movie changes the point of view of the camera, and yet, while the action is taking place and I continue to be one of the main characters, I can grasp the perspective of the audience and see the action from additional angles.

In this way the practice of sitting has started to produce unexpected benefits in my ability to handle difficult conversations and situations. Although I can't say exactly when it became evident or what the steps were along the way, I can clearly see a difference in my personality, pre-meditation and post-meditation. I can't always predict what will happen next or what unexpected benefits will reveal themselves for students who begin practicing, and I am reluctant to hold up such prizes as "You'll be able to be less reactive in difficult communications," because such prizes can easily become a distraction from the practice for practice's sake. It could be that the prize I claim from meditation is determined by what I most need to achieve, whereas yours will match your needs. I clearly needed to be less reactive in communication, and the world is a happier place around me as a result of this change.

When this shift I referred to above happens in my mind, I seem to become more skillfully able to speak the way I say I want to speak, make decisions in a more conscious manner, and generally be present to what is happening around me with more alertness. I appear to be less anxious about not knowing what will happen next, a matter that used to steal enormous resources from me in the form of worry, worst-case scenario appraisals, and planning. None of this improvement in communication was a planned goal of starting to meditate. I'm not sure anymore what it was I was expecting when I started practicing. I mentioned earlier that "being more spiritual" was high on the list. I had read about altered states of mind and even fantastic accounts of enhanced awareness that were certainly of interest to me.

But what I wasn't prepared for was the extraordinary ordinariness of what happens after sitting in meditation for an hour, and after sitting for many hours spread over years. What happened was that everyday life became amazing to watch as an observer, routine communications became festivals of nuances and theretofore unseen possibilities—all kinds of subtleties developed in terms of being aware of the world. The altered states of mind I had read about in which the meditator departed from their body, and similar supernormal events, became metaphors describing a very natural and normal state of mind in which I sometimes felt like I was both in my body and out of it as an observer.

Meditation, I learned, makes a person more conscious, more connected to life, more responsible and more present in their body and in their world. The supernormal state of mind I was waiting for didn't happen; and what I hadn't expected to happen, did. I began to understand what living wide-awake might be like.

The meditation teacher Cheri Huber wrote a helpful book titled *Nothing Happens Next*. I carry the title of that book around in my mental pocket as a mantra, a reminder to practice not so much to arrive somewhere or to get something, but more because practicing is a beautiful thing to do. I practice with a growing trust that what must develop and happen next will do so not because I forcefully *intend* it to happen, but because the nature of the practice is to bring forward that which *must* and wants to happen in the person practicing. I practice because it is what I do, like giving or studying or contributing service to the community. Whether I practice or not, life goes on, but now, having practiced, I am aware of the difference in me between when I act *with* meditation practice, and when I act *without* meditation practice.

Now that I know a little more about what's in the practice of meditation, I can't pretend to not know. I realize I don't have to practice, because there isn't any spiritual obligation to do so, at least none that I am part of. However, because I know the difference between a meditating me and a me who doesn't meditate, it becomes increasingly difficult to feel authentic and responsible without a meditation practice.

It's an awe-inspiring responsibility to be able to choose between practice and not practice. And as much as meditation has contributed to my life, not every conversation I have is conducted with perfect mindfulness; some interactions continue to catch me, trigger my reactivity. The difference is that afterward, when in cool quietness again, and I look back at how I conducted myself, I am more acutely aware of the departure from kindness than I was before I began meditating. Meditation has allowed me to become clear that I value kindness above all things, by granting me clear access as an observer to moments when I am not acting kindly.

TRY THIS

Listen for the Music's Sake

For the next seven days, use the time you normally set aside for meditation to listen to music. Try not to do anything else while you listen. Sit in your usual place at the usual time and listen to music of your choice. Try to assign no expectations to what will come from the practice so that whatever wants to happen next may do so without hindrance.

Try to select instrumental music so that you are not drawn to the specific message of the lyrics.

Make a Cup of Tea

Making a cup of tea is one of those things that can be done without much thought. Everything involved in the process is familiar and takes hardly any attention to accomplish. Try mixing things up by diverting all your available attention to each action involved in making a cup of tea. Let everything, from the moment of the decision to make the cup of tea, to the preparation of the place where it will be consumed, to the selection of the cup, all receive your full attentive consideration. In this way, when you are doing each action, you can take time to look carefully at the objects involved and to pay attention to sensations such as textures, room temperatures, ambient sounds.

Contrary to popular wisdom that a watched kettle doesn't boil, when watched, a kettle boils beautifully indeed. Let the kettle take as long as it needs to boil and watch it all the while, noticing how the steam begins to trail out of the spout and how sounds change as the water changes. Watch the kettle boil and notice any movement that takes place in the kettle when the water is at a full rolling boil. Selecting the cup and other utensils can receive more attention, too. Rather than reaching in for the first cup on the shelf, take time to notice if there are differences in all those cups that are supposed to be the same. Or, if you are one of those people who collects single mugs, take time to examine available mugs for the right one for this occasion. Smell the tea. Fold the cloth. Put everything away that isn't necessary before consuming the tea. Wait for the tea to steep and watch the color of the water changing, if you can see it.

Tick, Tock

How do you increase your focus in meditation? I asked a friend. "I use the tick-tock of a pesky clock in my home, which could be a distraction, but because I integrate it into my practice, it becomes a tool. My way of dealing with it is to count the ticks until they become too fast for my slowing-down mind and I miss a count. When that happens, I start counting again, and again I'll skip a tick when my awareness is slower than the clock's ticks. This usually happens around count fifty. When it does, I start again. After a while I reduce my counting to every third tick, and then to every fourth tick. By the time I get to landing on every fifth or sixth tick, I have the sensation of launching off one tick to float through time till I touch down on the next one, just like an astronaut playing on the moon." Try counting the ticks of a clock and see how you can slow your thoughts.

KEYS:

1. Taking a break in your practice schedule is helpful now and then.

2. Trying different meditation exercises now and then is helpful.

Food for Thought—Something Remains Present

Another powerful benefit meditation has brought into my life is that of becoming aware of how magnificently complex human minds are. I have learned that there are layers of awareness in my own mind and in the minds of fellow meditators. Noticing the *layeredness* of their own mind represents a significant milestone in the journey of inward watching. I find it difficult to describe this to students, yet people who practice will nod knowingly— even when my words aren't accurately describing the awareness that there is something in us that remains present and observing whether or not we meditate, coming into sharper focus when we do practice. Whether I'm sitting quietly or dancing, there continues to be something in me that does the witnessing, or noticing, and it is constantly available.

Sometimes, however, that witnessing mind is drowned out, seemingly, or pressed back into a corner like a quiet-spoken guest at a rowdy cocktail party, until someone announces who that guest is and attention is directed by curiosity to the newcomer. Through the practice of meditation, it seems that I can make space for the witnessing mind, and that is important because to me it is the wisest, kindest, and most aware part of my entire being. I think of that mind as the part of me that is already deeply integrated with everything. It is in that state of mind that I experience myself as being part of all that is. Its nature is harmonious, so it doesn't engage in battle with the more boisterous thoughts that sometimes occupy the ordinary mind that takes care of business day to day; it already knows how to be peaceful and doesn't need training to do what its nature is to do.

This has become a treasured realization, that I have within me something that prevails regardless of the noise of life. Even if I abandon it, when I return, it is in the same state of peaceful wisdom that it always was. Meditating has helped me understand anew the meaning of old loved hymns like Robert Wadsworth Lowry's "How Can I Keep from Singing," in which he writes:

> *My life flows on in endless song;*
> *above earth's lamentation . . .*
> *Thro' all the tumult and the strife*
> *I hear the music ringing.*

After meditating for some time, I became sidetracked and abandoned the practice for a while. When I started it up again, I expected to have to work hard to regain the consistency of practice and access to my quiet-mind that I had enjoyed before. I was surprised that a few days after beginning my practice again everything appeared to be exactly where I had left it, and I continued to have access to the flowing song of my life. When not practicing, that melody seems drowned out by lamentations of every kind. I learned that no matter how long I have sojourned in a tumultuous land, the return is swift and sometimes immediate. In Psalm 139 (NIV), I read:

> *Where can I go from your Spirit? Where can I flee*
> *from your presence? If I go up to the heavens, you*
> *are there; if I make my bed in the depths, you are*
> *there.*

It reminds me of the sweet welcome I feel, as if from the meditation practice itself, when after a long period of abandonment I return and everything I left behind is intact. This new awareness has, I believe, revealed in my life fresh resiliency, stronger courage, and hope that I believe I was unaware of before I practiced meditation.

5

MAY I INTERRUPT YOU?

Little by little, through patience and repeated effort,
the mind will become stilled in the Self.

BHAGAVAD GITA 6:24

Here's Your Reminder

Meditation is the practice of regularly sitting and observing the inner world of thought. The benefits of this practice include a reduction of reactivity and anxiety, and an increase in confidence when making decisions, as well as an increase in courage and resiliency. At least that describes my experience when regularly practicing. What would have been excellent, and would have probably maximized these beneficial results, would be if I could stay connected to the peaceful state of mind I experience during and directly after meditation. However, later in the day when navigating through the world—for example, dealing with a stressful situation or experiencing any number of ordinary communications—those beautiful moments of quiet would oftentimes seem forgotten.

In *How to Live in the World and Still Be Happy* by Hugh Prather, I discovered a handy exercise that I have used and elaborated on for many years to assist me in staying connected to the calm mind of my meditation practice throughout the day. Today, smartphones, watches, or anything with a timer can be used to set an alert for an irregular time of the day, for example 10:07 a.m., to call your attention back to the restful stillness of quiet-mind. When I first encountered this exercise, not having any of the electronic devices available today, I literally carried my bedside alarm clock, the wind-up kind, in my briefcase. It would sound a terrible alarm at the set time—and when it did, it would wrestle my attention from wherever it was, making a dent in any fast and hot thinking I may have been engaged in so that I could pause and ask myself, "Where were you in thought during your meditation this morning?" Or, "What is your thinking like right now?"

Nowadays, I use a less alarming reminder on my smartphone that plays a soft harp arpeggio every hour. I don't do this every day, but when I do, it has the effect of returning my awareness regularly to a peaceful place. My phone does not allow me to set automatic repeating reminders, so I have to set each alarm anew after being reminded to pause and consider. This activity of resetting the phone is in itself a ritual practice that requires me to pause whatever activity I am engaged in, and I find the few moments dedicated to resetting it to be helpful in generating sustained awareness. Sometimes, if an alarm is not appropriate, I set the phone to vibrate silently in my pocket, so that even if I am in a meeting or on a telephone conference, when the hour announces itself I can instantly realign my thought to a more harmonious tone.

Things to Notice on the Way

As you become accustomed to having time in your life daily to court stillness and introspection, you may notice an increase in your desire to practice. You may notice that you have started to enjoy being on your own, perhaps more than you used to. I tell students this is because they will most likely start to enjoy being by themselves. I warn them too that they may go through a period in which they will feel less comfortable being with large groups of people, for example at a party, and when they do find themselves among large numbers of people, they can fully expect themselves to remain aware of the quietness inside, feeling a pull away from busyness and toward quietness.

My experience is that when people meditate, they start to enjoy their own company. For some, this is a radical development because they may not have felt comfortable being alone before. Now they discover that they may even look forward to that time alone. Some report that they experience an increase in their ability to feel genuine loving-kindness for others. Among the other benefits that appear as a result of developing a taste for time alone, I believe, is an increase in personal integrity. Because of the clarity that gradually emerges from becoming familiar with our inner lives, there will undoubtedly come a time when you will feel a simple lack of interest in conversations and transactions that depend on duplicity, and you will experience a stronger willingness to trust your values.

Interrupt the Flow

At one point in my life, I noticed the strong tendency in me to flee away from solitude and run toward conversations in which I could rehash whatever current story was occupying a place in my mind where peace would have been preferred. I noticed also that I appeared sometimes to have more confidence in the power of retelling the story of my discontent than I did in the power of stillness. It seemed that I was motivated to get another person enrolled into my point of view to validate my experience. Even though this path leads nowhere, I would take it time and time again, like an addicted gambler who thinks the next round will be the winning one.

Finally, noticing the emptiness of that approach, I decided to interrupt my tendency to run toward the agreement of others and to go instead in the direction of solitude, to keep my own company when distressed. It was something new and caused me some anxiety at first. One effective place I found my solitude was in a swimming pool, swimming laps; insulated by the water, I recommitted to silence with each turn of a lap. It wasn't wonderful at first, because my habit of rehashing my concern with others apparently could continue with an imaginary audience, and my mind-chatter was no less dissatisfying than it had been with real people. Until, that is, I gave it something to do. Having something to focus on during stressful times proved to be a valuable interruption to the regular flow of thought. I would leave a book of inspiring phrases at the end of the pool, and each time I completed a lap, I would consult it quickly, selecting a new phrase to repeat to myself as I swam again. To my astonishment, I started to swim many more laps than I usually did. Time was being altered.

My mood was certainly being altered. After my swimming was through, even though the world out there remained in the same condition it was in before I started swimming, my world inside was altered.

A Mind of Your Own

Another powerful metaphor I keep in mind is that of thoughts being like vehicles on a freeway. Imagine that each thought is a discrete unit, like cars on a freeway, each with different occupants, destinations, and history. Although the cars share the freeway, there is a space between each one. Imagine that there is a space, or more accurately an interval, between each of your thoughts. I know that it can be difficult to imagine this when thoughts seem to overlap and touch each other, stimulating secondary thoughts, but it could be that the space between thought isn't discernible because of the general fast pace of the mind. Meditation creates a type of alert restfulness that is experienced as slowing down, especially from the perspective of the observer. In the same way that a news traffic helicopter observes the flow of traffic and reports it to the station, the spaces between cars on the freeway are noticed by the observing mind when practicing meditation. The space between cars is empty, no occupants, no history, no destination, and no event. Imagine such an eventless place exists between your own thoughts.

Your mind may seem as busy as a freeway, and yet there is a mind in you that is as quiet as this imagined space between thoughts. When thoughts are moving at the speed of a busy freeway, choice is reduced to the average speed, and if moving fast enough, more and more attention must be assigned to the cars around the driver. A commute in the traffic can render a person exhausted. I don't recommend dropping attention from matters of safety, but for the sake of the metaphor, I recommend lingering in the space between thoughts, to test if hanging out in that state of mind is refreshing. Fast-moving thinking is also called "hot" thinking, as in "he is a hothead," prone to a fast, narrow range of options, and decisions that can initiate a chain reaction of similar thoughts. Think pileup on the freeway.

When I detect anger rising, if I catch it in time, I try to notice the speeding up of my thinking. I can't always stop the fast-paced thoughts, but I can apply what is as good as braking or gearing down is in a car by not acting and not speaking. I physically stand still if possible, and that alone helps me find my way back to the spaces between angry thoughts. If necessary, I will resurrect a familiar short phrase, such as those discussed earlier, to repeat silently. If I have developed a strong relationship with the phrase through meditation practice, it can have an immediate effect of restoring balance to my mind, which moments before felt like it was under the stimulus of external influences.

Practicing throwing on the brakes, in addition to not acting and not talking in heated moments, can be accomplished by developing the habit of sometimes mindfully doing one thing at a time, such as eating without watching television, reading, or any other activity at the same time. I enjoy a variety of stimuli and I love watching a good movie while having a good meal, and I also see the value of learning how to do something with a single mind, which I call concentration—all my attention is centered on the activity at hand. I acknowledge that, as enjoyable as the sum total experience of eating and watching a movie is, I may be losing out on something very special when I fail to concentrate from time to time on one single activity. "When you are walking, walk; when you are sitting, sit. Don't wobble"* are words that remind me to consider that whatever I find myself doing at any moment might as well have my undivided attention.

....

* Attributed variously to Gautama Buddha or Chinese Zen master Yúnmén Wényǎn.

TRY THIS

On Call

Enroll the participation of a friend or acquaintance who is willing to call you, or send you a text message, at three random times during this day to remind you to think about your meditation practice. When the call or message comes, all you have to do is pause and notice what you are currently doing. If you did meditate in the morning, try to remember that time of sitting. Then, go about your business as usual.

Delayed Response

Write a series of e-mail reminders to yourself and schedule them for later delivery to your in-box. Set them to arrive at random times over the next several weeks. Let the messages contain a simple question that calls you back to peace, such as "What could you be thinking right now?" "Send Later" features are available to Microsoft Outlook users under the "Options" tab in the "Compose message" dialogue box by selecting "Delay delivery"; other e-mail servers, such as Gmail, can be set up to do the same through add-on applications such as Right Inbox, which offers ten free scheduled e-mails per month.

KEYS:

1. Interrupting your thought routine will help you understand your inner life.

2. Little by little, through patience and repetition, you will become better and better at your practice.

Food for Thought—The Mystery of the Shiva Temple

I once had the experience of interrupting my busy-mind inadvertently by being immersed in sensory overload. In 2007, I visited an ashram in Varanasi, India. The guru sent me to visit the main Shiva temple with a guide, Tejpal. Up until a recent time, the temple was accessible only to Hindu-born Hindus. Now it has been decided that no one has exclusive access to God and the temple is open to anyone. The son of the man who built the Taj Mahal went on a conversion mission to convert India to Islam, and one of his strategies was to tear down major Hindu temples and erect mosques in their place, just like the Romans did with pagan temples when expanding the Roman Empire. Half of the Shiva temple remains and half is a mosque. The Shiva temple is one of the most ancient and important in India and was recently threatened with bombing, so security was naturally heightened. I was searched eight times and went through three metal detectors. I was watched constantly by teams of armed men, which contributed to my heightening sense of anxiety. No one escaped their scrutiny and somehow, like everything in Varanasi, it all worked together in a maddening, frenzied, elegant, and free-flowing movement, like cells flowing in a bloodstream. There were so many people, so much going on, so much noise, so much to see, that I was awestruck into a kind of calm silence. My guide asked, "Are you OK?"

"Yes, I am happy," I offered with a smile.

He smiled back. "Ah, you feel the something-special-holy! We all feel it here."

My throat constricted with unbidden emotion and recognition of the subtle something-holy that is bleeding out of every three-thousand-year-old stone step that mothers and their children are touching with reverence, because every inch of this place is holy ground. I shuffled along shoeless in the human ant column through filthy water, flower-strewn floors, and shallow, dark, congested tunnels . . . till at last I came to *the* place. I think there is a lingam* at the center, but I don't know. I couldn't see through the tears, and the ancient pit and its content is covered with garlands and garlands and garlands and yogurt and honey and water and I don't know what else. There was only a moment to kneel and touch the water as hoards of devotees clamored behind, waiting to embrace the energy at the center where, it is believed, the lord of change and renewal is highly likely to meet your heart's request.

I can barely remember the rest of the journey. When did I get that red dot on my head? How did I get my shoes and camera back? I know we left them outside with security, where we purchased garlands and offerings and gifts to take back to the guru as sign of our pilgrimage.

There were other temples, shops, and rickshaw rides, eggs to buy, bags of sugar with ants crawling around inside (causing no one any distress), and crafty dodging of police as the guide overloaded the auto rickshaw. And we laughed.

....

* The word "lingam" in Sanskrit refers to a mark or sign in the form of a smooth and rounded pillar of stone varied in size and shape. It is intended to represent the deity Shiva and is used in temples for worship as a symbol of divine creative energy.

And the guide held my hand for a moment and smiled with silent understanding.

Earlier that day, a staff member at the ashram told me about the sad changes she had noticed in Varanasi over the last ten years. She told me about her concern that this incredible mystery on the earth would slip away. She told me about the fast-food chain that opened and was so successful that they took in enough money in one week to open a second and they have plans for more. Fast food in Varanasi? What could that be compared to? I can't imagine.

Everywhere I looked in Varanasi, I saw life as incomprehensibly complex and diverse as I could ever imagine. So fast and so intense that I couldn't integrate it quickly enough. Badly broken systems, beautiful brave beggars, dark-eyed God-crazy sages, and God, that which remains already and always present, everywhere.

Back at the Ashram Seva, a little bit of the temple still lingered in me as I sat and listened to the guru talk to us about the importance of Seva (selfless service to others). He explained that some people serve to complete themselves, to fill emptiness within. He explained that *sadana* (spiritual practice) is what fills us, and when we are full, there is an overflow, and that overflow when directed to others and worthwhile pursuits constitutes Seva.

"But," he said, "anywhere is good to start."

6

CONSIDER THIS . . .

But when you move amidst the world of sense, free from attachment and aversion alike, there comes the peace in which all sorrows end, and you live in the wisdom of the Self.

BHAGAVAD GITA 2:64

Short Span of Attention

I playfully tell my friends that I have a short span of attention and that they should think twice about asking me to help with a project such as painting a room, for example— that is, unless they want each wall to be a different color and as long as they don't mind if I do not complete the task in the time allotted because I will most likely find an interesting book on their shelf to read. I am encouraged by how many people identify with this characteristic. Some have been led to believe, like I have, that it is a flaw of concentration that will impede progress in spiritual practices such as meditation. You're supposed to be able to stay focused and to be one-pointed in your attention. All the while, life around us is designed for multitasking, and advertisements are measured out in short bites of information, queued back-to-back. Product placements in movies bombard us with messages to motivate us, all the while we are following a story and plotline. I no longer feel embarrassed about my shortened span of attention, and I don't let it stop me from designing a meditation practice that takes me beyond distractions into pure uninterrupted periods of peaceful-mind. I take comfort in the formula of regular practice without attachment to how it should be.

Because I thrive with a lot of stimulation and I enjoy many options to choose from, I found that meditating on a passage is particularly helpful and enjoyable. You're going to need a passage of writing you find inspiring: a prayer or poem to try it out for yourself. The engaging part of this practice, for someone like me who demands a lot of stimulation, is that in this exercise I get to think about every single word in the selected text until I am finished and ready to move on to the next one. That may take a long while, or it may be completed relatively quickly. Thinking about every single word is an exercise in creativity, because when I land on a pronoun or another simple word, I tend to want to move on to the next, hopefully more substantial, word to think about. But instead of moving on, I pause on the word "a," for example, and think about it. How it sounds, what it means in our language, what other words could substitute for it, and so on. Then I go on.

For example, if I select Psalm 23, "The Lord is my shepherd . . . ," the first word I get to think about is "the." I typically ask myself what it means and I give myself adequate time to ramble on, " 'The' means not just any, but 'the,' a specific something . . ." Sometimes I don't have anything to say, so I just listen to the sound of the word in my mind's ear. I don't mind if my attention wanders. If I notice it has, I let myself come back to the passage and move to the next word: "Lord." I ask myself again, "What does this word mean to you?" I may find myself thinking about gender-neutral language trends and wondering what a gender-neutral substitute for the word "Lord" might be. I might find myself thinking about images of older cultures and concepts of loyalty and chivalry. I try to ask myself what the word means in the context of this passage and dwell on that for a while. When it is time, I move to the following word: "is."

This way, I am spending time with the passage, but in a

unique and creative way. My experience is that the practice instills both deep contemplative silence as well as a profound personal relationship with the words of the text I chose. Sometimes, I select only a single phrase for this practice. Other times, I select a significant poem, like a poem of Rumi, or a different psalm, and consider the meaning one phrase or sentence at a time. It is also useful to work with a passage that I have committed to memory, although it is as useful to have a book open, with my finger on the phrase or work I am focusing on. This helps maintain my focus on the process. I have noticed that when I work with memorized passages, I can find myself taking a left turn away from the assigned path, momentarily forgetting where I was or what it was I was doing.

Observe and Report

I have often heard the phrase "Let us turn within" spoken by someone drawing a group's attention to prayer or meditation. One of my teachers would ask students who used the phrase what they meant by "within." I think he was making the point that mindfulness, or sacredness, or the Presence, or consciousness, is available to us everywhere and to be careful not to create a separation between inner life and outer life. In the ordinary moments of life, too, whether our eyes are open or shut, whether the environment is quiet or not, there remains an opportunity to be tuned in to inner life. It would be wonderful if we could always have access to a sanctuary or a quiet garden, or to the ocean or our meditation spot with candles and a CD playing flute music. More commonly though, the times we need peace the most, none of these may be immediately available.

For example, one day I returned from a run around the lake with a friend of mine. We returned to my house to have some coffee, exhilarated by the physical exercise and elevated by our time together in nature, when all of a sudden a giant lizard ran over his foot. My cat had brought it in and it had been hiding, planning its escape. My friend yelled in alarm, and in an instant peace was gone from both of us. We began the process of searching the house for the giant lizard that in my mind now seemed to have fangs. Occupying every space in my awareness was the question "Where is it?" There was no thought to turning within; that was not interesting to me right then.

In reality, there was nothing in that scenario that was preventing me from practicing inner peace, and it would have likely been the very best thing for me to do. I could quite easily have nurtured peace by practicing being an interested observer of life as it was happening around me and still taken care of the search at the same time—possibly even more effectively than when possessed with exaggerated images of the size and danger of the gentle lizard.

I heard about a movie called *Observe and Report* when one of the young people in my life brought it over for an evening of movies. Although I wouldn't have selected the title by myself, I found something humorous and helpful in it. The story is about a bipolar mall security guard who is not supposed to take any action at the mall when an incident happens. Because he is not a police officer, he is not required by his employer to do anything that he is not trained to do. Though I didn't watch the movie with the young people, I got to thinking how I sometimes attempt to do things that are not rightly mine to do. A good example for me is making judgements, correcting others, sharing unnecessary opinions. Life turns out to be so much more enjoyable when I observe without thinking it necessary to comment.

Influenced by the title of this movie, I began an experiment in which for a while I adopted a friendly attitude toward life, as if I were entertaining a happy secret, and went about my business with an effortless smile. My secret mission was to be a keen observer, trying to notice as much as possible in one day how much peacefulness is available everywhere. I noticed how many opportunities there were to fill in information and meaning, and as I withheld the inclination to do so, my movement through the day became like a daylong meditation practice and turned out to be really pleasant. I remember making a stop-motion video with a friend who had purchased a new webcam and wanted to try out the feature that allowed him to take one frame, change the scene, and take another frame. We set up the camera to focus on him sitting on a couch with a blanket on his lap. We took one frame, then moved the blanket and took the second frame, advancing in this way until the blanket had moved over his head.

When we were done, the finished video of separate frames delighted us as the blanket appeared to move magically over him. It was interesting to see how we fill in the spaces between frames so that we can make sense of the sequential images, turning separate photos into a fluid movie. In between the separate images are spaces of nothingness. In life, I notice the tendency, and I'm glad I have it, to fill in the blank spaces, and I'm learning to be mindful of how I do that. I notice some circumstances when it may not be necessary to do so at all. For example, adding meaning to an action. He did that, or she said that, or I no longer have this and it means the other.

I think of going within as referencing the empty spaces where there is no such added meaning and where I could let things be as they are. I began to practice going within more frequently during regular activities beyond my time of sitting in meditation in the morning. In so doing, I began to think of meditation not only as an activity I engaged in each morning but also as an approach to life that reached beyond the time I set aside for being still. The more I sat in meditation in the morning, the more the attitude of meditation stayed with me through the day, allowing me to observe the world around me and notice the style in which I was engaging it. I became aware of a reduction in my tendency to add meaning when none is required, and also of the emergence of a kind-hearted interest in life.

Bombarded with Information

Lyall Watson, in *Beyond Supernature*, describes how raw information of every kind descends on everything on earth in an endless stream of energy in the form of material and rays from sources we cannot observe, including X-rays and infrared rays, radio waves, microwaves, and more.* Much of this information makes little impact on us while we tend to the ordinary matters of our lives, trying to communicate well, trying to live a compassionate life, trying to make a contribution to the lives of others, and trying to understand our place in the scheme of things.

....

* Lyall Watson, *Beyond Supernature: A New Natural History of the Supernatural* (New York: Bantam, 1986), p. 85.

It's a good thing that there is a system of filtering out information that apparently we do not need so that we are not overwhelmed and so that we can attend to living while focusing on what is important. Our senses are able to process only a narrow band of information that represents the visible and audible spectrum. This tiny opening we call "reality." To make matters even more interesting, we interpret and restrict even the little bit of information we do have access to.

The reality we perceive is not all there is "out there." At least that's what experiments on frogs' eyes suggest. It seems that frogs have eyes that have features in common with ours. Theoretically, they should be able to see as well as we do. However, microelectrodes implanted in the frog's eyes reveal that only select bits of information are being passed on from the eye to the frog's brain. From the richness of the visual world, only very basic kinds of messages are being relayed to the frog.

> *The frog does not seem to see or, at any rate, is not concerned with the detail of stationary parts of the world around him. He will starve to death surrounded by food if it is not moving.**

....

* J. Y. Lettvin, H. R. Maturana, W. S. McCulloch, and W. H. Pitts, "What the Frog's Eye Tells the Frog's Brain," chap. 7 in *The Mind: Biological Approaches to Its Functions*, William C. Corning and Martin Balaban, eds. (New York: Interscience Publishers, 1968), pp. 233–58.

I wonder sometimes if we are much different from the frogs in this regard. Of all the information we have available, we simply do not take it all in. But we constantly make decisions based on the restricted look we have of the world through the tiny slit we call reality when there is apparently much more available. For example, have you ever decided to buy a new car? A friend might ask you, "Have you considered buying a red Jeep?"

"A red Jeep?" you say. "I've never really seen a red Jeep."

"Oh, look, there is one right now parked outside your home."

You like it, and you decide absentmindedly to notice Jeeps. Because you do begin to notice Jeeps, all of a sudden the world becomes filled up with Jeeps. It is as if the universe heard you were interested in Jeeps and suddenly started production. Of course, they were always there, you just weren't noticing them.

We are sophisticated beings. Working within the narrow range of sensory information we receive, we can tune out anything we do not want to know, and tune in on the strangest things. Like when we walk into a room and a clock is ticking really loudly, but after a while we tune out the sound. It doesn't stop. We just do not hear it anymore. We reduce the slit through which we see our world, and our reality inside changes. But on the outside, things are just as they always were.

I've heard this technique of perceiving described as "cocktail party awareness." When we are at a party, we hear only the conversation we are engaged in, until someone on the other side of the room says our name and, *whoosh*, our attention is dragged to the place from where our name came.

The next time you sit to meditate, tune your attention to hear the sounds around you in a new, focused way by paying attention to every sound that falls on your ears. If it is possible, sit outside where you will have access to a variety of environmental sounds that are typically tuned out and become a backdrop to information we label more important. With eyes closed, let yourself begin to pay attention to your immediate environment and listen for sounds. No matter your location, let your hearing seek out sounds near you, and then the sounds a little farther away from you and again farther away than that. Without straining to hear anything, let yourself be available to the sounds of life.

Whom Do You Aspire to Be Like?

The Dalai Lama writes that there are two basic types of meditation: analytical and stabilizing (or subjective and objective meditation).* The difference is in focus. With analytical or subjective meditation, the focus is on cultivating awareness or developing understanding. For example, examining or exploring the accuracy of an idea about life, or purposefully cultivating an attitude of gratitude by reviewing what you appreciate in your life and paying attention to the feelings that arise when you think about that gratitude.

With stabilizing meditation, you fix your attention on something, like the flame of a candle, or an image of someone you revere, or the quality of your breath as it passes in and out of your lungs. He also describes meditating in the "manner of wishing," giving the example of such wishing "to be filled with the compassion of a Buddha." Also, he suggests that you can "go one step further, into *imagination meditation*," in which you envision that you have qualities that you actually do not have yet. Focusing your attention on qualities you aspire to, as a form of meditation, is powerful, in that what is in your attention regularly tends to influence your thought, decision-making process, words, and actions. In other words, you may find yourself becoming like that which occupies a prominent position in your awareness.

....

* Dalai Lama, *How to Practice: The Way to a Meaningful Life* (New York: Pocket Books, 2002).

You can identify qualities you aspire to by examining the people in your life whom you admire. Make a list of the top ten influential people in your life right now. Under each person's name, write the values or qualities that each person exhibits—for example, honesty, kindness, directness, etc. Try to come up with one- or two-word values (loving-kindness, patience) rather than a phrase (she is kind to animals). Take your time completing the exercise, even if it takes a couple of days to do so. When it is complete, transfer the list of values/qualities to a separate page. I like to do this on my computer, where I can sort the resulting list in alphabetical order. This gives me insight into how frequently a particular word surfaced in my list of qualities.

I then delete those qualities that receive only one mention, and with the remaining list of qualities, I assign myself the task of ranking it from most significant to least significant. For the purpose of my meditation exercise, I then take the top three or four qualities and use them over the next thirty days in the following way: If the first quality on my final list is loving-kindness, then on day one at my regular meditation time, I sit with the quality and consider it in the style of the Dalai Lama's imagination meditation. I give myself the assignment of imagining how I would show up in the world if I were an excellent role model of loving-kindness. I imagine being responsible for teaching what loving-kindness means to others and what curriculum I might devise to accomplish that. I examine where I have shown loving-kindness in my life and what one thing I could do today to bring loving-kindness into more prominence in my life.

If the second word on my list is honesty, I do the same meditation exercise focusing on honesty on day two, and on day three I do the same thing with the third word on the list. Then on day four, I begin again with loving-kindness and carry on until thirty days have passed.

TRY THIS

Select seven poems or prayers that have meaning for you. You might need some time to prepare. Try to have all seven pieces selected and available at your place of meditation so that you can go to your task easily and without fuss. Each day, sit with your selected writing and review silently the meaning of each word. If you have a time constraint, don't be concerned if you do not get through the entire text. Also, if you determine halfway that you have had enough, simply complete what you're doing, sit quietly for a few moments, and continue again the next day with the next piece of writing.

KEYS:

1. Shifting your mental focus for a while to inspiring writing helps unlock new depths of meaning in the words not easily accessed on the surface.

2. Memorizing inspiring words will help you easily refer to them as needed and can serve as an anchor in your mind for inner peace.

Food for Thought—Untapped Resources

We have so much available to us, so many untapped resources that we have yet to discover. There is so much more we could let through the slit we call reality, if we only knew how. And when we do know how, we can make our personal world so much brighter. *Peanuts* cartoonist Charles M. Schulz said, "Life is like a ten-speed bike, most of us have gears we never use."

I have found meditation to be an effective means to learn how to use all the gears of awareness, because in the quietness I have been able to observe how loyal I am to certain narrow ranges of information and responses. If you accept the invitation given above to experiment with sitting and listening in a way that you haven't done before, you may discover how full the world is of sounds you hadn't noticed, especially if your awareness has been arrested by urgent stressful thoughts. By sitting quietly I became aware of how easy it is for me to focus down on something to the point that it looms over me and displaces any of the other information that is available to me, information that remains unavailable because of my narrow focus. Certain types of ideas capture my attention (when I'm not being mindful) more powerfully than others. Thoughts that cause stress or worry or that seem urgent are strongest in this ability. Yet if I sit long enough with them in the sanctuary of my quiet-mind, they often lose their grip and give way to untapped resources of calm wisdom.

You've got six months to live; you're not suited to this job; the job market is tough now; you're too old for this position; you're too young to understand; you'll never dance again. Worrisome ideas like these have provided me with powerful focus opportunities during my meditation practice. I have found it useful to sit with such thoughts, whether they are accurate or not, and consider them. Sometimes I have to let them run their course and exhaust their worst-case scenarios, until at last there is quietness enough to hear what has not yet been heard.

That is what I think of when I read Krishna's words "the wisdom of the Self" as opposed to the wisdom of the self. The Self to me is the untapped resource, the additional gears, the capacity we have to live in this world without being governed by it. And I believe it is available under or beyond the realm of surface-level mental activity, in a quietness that is accessible through meditation.

7

WRITING MEDITATION

Wherever the mind wanders, restless and diffuse in
its search for satisfaction without, lead it within; train
it to rest in the Self.

BHAGAVAD GITA 6:26

How I Discovered Writing as a Meditative Practice

In the Bhagavad Gita, Prince Arjuna is exasperated by his own busy-mind and likens his attempts at controlling thinking to trying to change the direction the wind blows. Reassured that such great seekers as Prince Arjuna have faced challenges similar to what I was facing, I more easily abandoned trying to make my thinking do anything at all. Like a child needing attention, or a cat insisting on being patted upon demand, once I yielded to what my thinking was doing, it seemed to settle down all by itself.

I say that I began "watching my thinking" because I haven't found a better way to describe what began to be my daily meditation practice. First thing in the morning, after making my body comfortable, I would sit, either in my bed propped up with pillows or in my living room in a comfortable chair.

At first, I would make a cup of coffee before sitting and later experimented by observing the difference between sitting with and without coffee. Without coffee, I would sometimes doze off, so I settled into a practice of setting my brewer to begin its job ten minutes before my scheduled meditation time. To this day, the smell of morning coffee makes me think of meditation and those peaceful moments when I began practicing years ago.

I would set a timer, but I would set no expectations or agenda. I began with a modest ten minutes and approached the exercise with an explorer's curiosity: What will I find here today? I practiced paying attention to what happened when I sat and closed my eyes. I began to notice something: I was aware that I was paying attention to my thinking. I was aware that there were several layers of mental activity going on in there, and I became aware of just how fast it was all happening in there, sometimes too fast for me to keep pace with what was going on. There were two things going on, thinking and watching thinking. Each activity seemed independent, each with its own temperament; and one, thought, was traveling very, very fast and appeared to be beyond the reach of any control whatsoever. The other, observing, was calmer and seemed already to know how to be peaceful.

A thought would land on a topic and in a split second that thought splintered into multiple other directions, like a getaway bouncy-ball ricocheting against walls in a vast hall—and I was not able to predict its next landing place or know if it would ever stop. Once a thought was headed in a certain direction, there didn't seem to be a dependable way to retrieve the thought or edit it. It was not similar to reading a student's homework assignment, where thoughts were captured on paper, frozen in time, when they were confined, one hoped, to a single topic and could be tweaked, edited, and even deleted if necessary. I began to notice there were thoughts that I could imagine spending more time with, or possibly even gently leading them back to accuracy, but I had no way to do so because my mind was already elsewhere.

It occurred to me that if I actually wanted to "observe" my thoughts, I might consider writing some of them down. At first, writing didn't seem to have anything to do with meditation. Remembering to be flexible and to maintain an explorer's attitude, and remembering also my resolve to create a practice that worked for me, I put aside the hesitation and began to write down some thoughts that appeared during meditation.

My morning sitting now had something new: a blank journal and my favorite pen close at hand. At first I would write down only a thought or two when I noticed one I wanted to examine. I would commit each thought gently to a place where I could look at it serenely and unhurriedly because I had written it down. But then, I enjoyed the practice so much that I started to write and write and write. I paid no mind to grammar, spelling, complete sentences, or making any sense out of the words. I just wrote; and although the thoughts coming through my pen to the paper continued to be disconnected and range over a vast territory of topics, I noticed that they had been slowed down to what I heard someone describe as "the speed of write."

Not until I actually wrote my thoughts down did I understand what doors of insight writing could open for me. Now I had something more practical to add to meditation, I could slow some thoughts down and preserve them on paper where I could look at them at leisure. I had gradually become aware that I was able to observe my inner life, but I didn't know what to do about it. Now I discovered that by taking a mental snapshot of what was in there in the form of the rambling words I committed to paper, I could take a new look at my thoughts, and things started to become clearer.

Frozen on the Page

My morning sessions took on a new tone and left me feeling profoundly contemplative and peaceful, the same sensation I felt after a deep, slow yoga class.

Additionally, I noticed something that amazed me. I wanted, and needed, more time than the fifteen minutes I had set for my practice, I needed and wanted time for both sitting and writing. That in itself was a miracle. I had not predicted wanting to do more meditation. Perhaps because no one was making me do it, and no one was expecting a particular response from me, I felt drawn in by the curiosity of what was coming up in the writing.

Freed in this way, I was able to become fascinated with what I now believe is the "heart" of my meditation: the practice of noticing, and it took slowing some ideas down to paper for me to notice them and what influence they were working in me.

I began to notice themes emerge in my writing, and my endless thought-world seemed to be merely variations on some basic themes. An internal pattern or order was beginning to show itself in that chaos of blazing activity. Once I began to notice repeated themes, I could follow and release thoughts as belonging to a category, and more important, I began to realize that much of the inner real-estate was occupied by a very narrow range of concerns. I began to become excited about the prospect of introducing a new or different category of thought and to choose to think about what I wanted to think about.

I increased my meditation time modestly as needed, and eventually set aside enough time to read what I had written, a practice that opened an ocean of understanding and deep growth for me. There on the page, frozen in time and space, I was able to observe a small slice of the information superhighway of my mind.

Once observed in this way, I began to be able to sort out the difference between certain types of thoughts: accurate thoughts, exaggerated thoughts, unkind thoughts, compassionate thoughts, fearful thoughts, creative thoughts, innocent thoughts, and confused thoughts.

I didn't do anything about it. I just practiced noticing. After a while, I settled into writing regularly, frequently turning to my journal in times when I wanted to take a close, unhurried look at the content of my mind.

Go Slower

Through writing in a meditative way, I relearned the power of "go slower." Between the windows at the east end of the corridor in the Library of Congress is a quotation from Francis Bacon's *Essays*: "Reading maketh a full man; conference a ready man; and writing an exact man." In particular, writing by hand, being slow to perform, can have the effect of perfecting focus and organizing thought. Typing, although faster than writing, with care it can have similar beneficial effects of contributing to clarity because the pace is slower than thought and with the slower pace introspection is possible.

In *Light on the Yoga Sūtras of Patañjali*, B. K. S. Iyengar writes, "Through introspection comes the end of pain and ignorance." Creating space around fast-moving thoughts has allowed me to reduce the number of actions and decisions that lead to self-induced pain or that can harm others because they were founded on fast-moving, sometimes reactive, sometimes inaccurate thoughts.

Follow Your Intuition

Writing as a meditative practice can help us to get in touch with our intuition, which is important to people who want to live a more conscious life. I think of intuition as inner wisdom that can act as a compass to guide us through life's ups and downs when we maintain a close and personal relationship with it. Meditative writing is well suited to bringing out the guidance of intuition because of its slow, introspective tone.

Whenever I talk to people about the voice of intuition inside them, the issue arises of how to recognize it; how to sort it out from every other kind of voice that emerges from within. Then there is another, second challenge, and that is when we *do* recognize the truth-filled voice of intuition but we ignore it or do exactly the opposite and continue with what we wanted to do in the first place. Using your journal meditatively can be a tool to both recognize your inner voice and help you to follow it.

When themes, phrases, or ideas repeat in your meditative writing, consider looking at them more closely as possible intuitive nudges from within. I don't have an exact method for sorting intuition from other internal voices; however, I have this notion that inner wisdom has a personality that is characterized by nonviolence and calm-ness. If the repeating ideas are critical in nature, or com-pare you unfavorably to others, or are complaining in tone, they are still worth examining but I wouldn't identify them as intuition. Nevertheless, intuitive urges may lead me to the edge of my comfort zone and invite me to do that which I know I must do but don't want to. Intuition, however, will not guide me to do something harmful or violent to myself or others.

If I do notice some line of thought in my meditative writing that fits the profile of possibly being intuition, I can follow it in small steps by asking myself, "What one thing can I do this week that will represent a step in the direction of this inner urge?" I take small steps in the direction of what I believe to be intuitive nudges rather than leap off into the unknown. This has been helpful in the cases where I have incorrectly identified something as intuition, be-cause the small step generates awkwardness or struggle and I am able to step back and reconsider.

In the case where I correctly identify the voice of intuition in my meditative writing but choose to ignore the prompting for whatever reason, a similar anxious response emerges in me, the kind of unease that goes with knowing I'm not doing what I ought to be doing.

Is It All Right to Feel That Good?

Another area where the slowed-down pace of meditative writing helped me was in uncovering spiritual concepts I had learned as a child that were affecting me below the surface of conscious thought.

Soon after beginning to write as part of meditation practice, I noticed recurring themes, such as a tendency to be uncomfortable with the feelings of peace and rightness I was experiencing through meditation. It didn't seem to be all right to feel that good, and I realized I was expecting some kind of equalizing event to take place to put me in my place. By examining the emerging themes in my writing, I discovered that I felt guilty about being happy. The themes didn't always emerge as actual words written on the page, but rather as thoughts and feelings while I was writing. Sometimes I would pause in the middle of a written sentence to notice my feelings. Because I did not rush through the pause, thoughts that were not fully formed yet had an opportunity to come into focus, and I was able to see what was disturbing me in them.

Although my early religious upbringing was fairly agreeable and what beliefs I had been taught were presented in the kindest of ways, I somehow had learned that the Creator frowned on anything other than struggle, suffering, and hard work. The concept was reinforced with the story of God sending His son to suffer on behalf of humanity. I had been listening to the story since I was a child, and now as an adult I was discovering how it shaped my attitude toward happiness. I wanted to avoid disappointing the Creator with too much self-generated happiness.

Merely identifying the worrisome thought helped to relieve the stress it was causing. I thought I might need to do something specific to remedy the situation, but instead, the act of discovering it seemed to be enough to shift my childlike loyalty to early religious stories, and I began to accept that it was a good thing to be deeply peaceful and happy.

8

GETTING UNSTUCK

When you let your mind follow the call of the senses,
they carry away your better judgement as storms
drive a boat off its charted course on the sea.

BHAGAVAD GITA 2:67

Encountering Blocks

When I sat and meditated, I would frequently reach a
point of deep inward quiet from which multiple new directions for me would become clear, and although I had a
growing confidence in the practice, I would sometimes
get stuck by slipping into worry and stress as easily as slipping into a favorite and well-worn sweater that is as comfortable as my own skin. At times like these I would feel
like the worry had carried away my better judgment, as

the Gita says, like a storm drives a boat off its charted course.

Although it wasn't apparent immediately, the thought storm and course confusion was often a result of my practice working on a deep level in my life, on the inside. For example, I might be meditating on a specific quality of being, such as loving-kindness, and below the surface of consciousness that quality becomes stimulated in such a way that everything in me that blocks its expression is brought to my attention to be dealt with.

It is as if blocks to that quality are forced out into the open where all I can do is deal with them or remain stuck. In this way, things can sometimes appear to be getting worse as a result of spiritual practice before they begin to get better.

I used to, and probably still can, get frustrated because I want things to move from zero to sixty in one second. I want to go from worried to carefree without the steps between those two domains. So when something presents itself that I experience as a block or a detour that delays my progress, I can feel thwarted and unwilling to continue.

Here is how it happens. If the quality of being I am meditating on is "mindful communication," or if I am contemplating more loving relationships in my family, it can happen that I begin to notice, oftentimes suddenly, all the difficulties in the existing relationship in various other areas of my life, for example at work or among friends. It is because that quality of mindful communication I am meditating on or praying about begins to take center stage in my awareness and seems to dislodge or bring to light everything in me that is incompatible with it.

I know now to take this kind of development as a sign that my spiritual practice is working. I notice now that when things get stirred up and I seem to be carried in the opposite direction of my intention, I respond with less panic. I don't take it as a death sentence anymore and am more likely to sit it out through meditation, and I try instead to adopt the attitude of "I wonder where this will go next?"

When this is happening, I watch closely because there is information in the dissonance that is stirred up through spiritual practice, information that can help me embody the quality I am meditating on, if I am willing to look deeply into it. Maybe it is because my communication style has been getting in the way of loving relationships at work and with friends, and now that I am courting loving relationships in my family, the area in my life where I am not engaged in mindful communication is shifted in front of me as a result of my meditation.

A long time ago I was interning at a spiritual organization. The director enrolled all the interns to bring the awareness of prosperity into their prayers and meditations on behalf of the organization. Things got worse financially, and eventually it was discovered that a member of the staff was embezzling money. We asked the director of the organization how this could happen, and she explained that it was precisely the working out of our prayers and meditations.

I have never forgotten that and take it to heart every time I think I am stuck or that my inner work is not taking me in the direction I think it should be. Sometimes what I interpret as being stuck or feeling empty or directionless is more an issue of being impatient with a process that takes time. It just isn't happening fast enough for me. I can, in these moments, find myself wanting to throw everything out and quit.

I heard from someone who was in Berlin when the wall came down. He said that for many people it was unbelievable that it happened, even though many of them had imagined such a day, or had prayed for it. This person said then that in his opinion, it couldn't have happened any other way, not at any other time, without violence, and that in his opinion all the prayers and intentions and whatever else contributed were being answered in that movement. Now when things don't move in my life, I think of that permanent-seeming wall and I sit still more patiently in meditation again. I take moments of no apparent movement as opportunities to dwell on what may be growing in me on the unseen side of my life. I take moments of dissonance as clues about what in me is preventing progress. I am learning that if I give up in moments of nonmovement or dissonance, I may be giving up too soon.

What to Do When Stuck

There are times when nothing seems to work, even for those engaged in regular meditation practice. They can enter into a period of dryness during which well-known methods seem as irritating as an insect bite on sunburned skin. Nothing seems to be moving, and it is difficult to make sense of it. What can you do to help yourself when this moment arrives? And what causes it? Sometimes the ambition to keep up a steady rhythm in our practice runs dry without warning. Sometimes the nature of sitting and contemplating produces temporary disorientation and the one practicing can briefly lose sight of the original inspiration for the journey. Sometimes the deep inquiry unsettles so much dust from the past that it appears to be preferable to cause no further waves of disturbance. Here are some suggestions for how to move gently through such moments of being stuck.

Consider Other Perspectives

In Roger von Oech's *A Whack on the Side of the Head* there is a wealth of practical advice for how to learn to think more creatively. One of the techniques I appreciate the most is to consider other right answers to solutions using creative thinking, which he describes as

> an outlook that allows you to search for ideas and play with your knowledge and experience. With this outlook, you try different approaches, first one, then another, often not getting anywhere. You use crazy, foolish and impractical ideas as stepping stones to practical new ideas. You break the rules occasionally, and explore for ideas in unusual outside places. In the end, your creative outlook enables you to come up with new ideas.*

....

* Roger von Oech, *A Whack on the Side of the Head: How You Can Be More Creative* (New York: Business Plus, 2008), p. 6.

During times of being spiritually stuck, I frequently get out Roger von Oech's book and creativity pack to help me get into a playful and creative mindset.

One such exercise that helps open the mind to other perspectives is to put unrelated ideas together and to look for possible connections between them. For example, if the question is "How do I become a more mindful communicator?" I might ask a friend—without telling them what the question is—to name a random item in their home or workplace. If they name a teapot, I thank them and apply that teapot to my question about mindful communication.

Then my task is to playfully write down in my journal, during my meditation practice time, as many ways as I can how a teapot is the answer to my question. Another similar perspective and broadening technique is to randomly open a book on your bookshelf, turn to a page, read the first complete sentence on that page, and take it as the answer to your question. Write it down at the top of a page in a journal and assign yourself the task of explaining the connection between the sentence and your issue. A playful attitude is important. I can't take this too seriously. The point is to crack open the stuckness and let some joyful and creative light in.

Stand Still and Do Nothing

When you are feeling stuck, especially if you feel mild anxiety about it, it could be that your mind is telling you a story about what that stuckness means. Standing still metaphorically means to do nothing about your stuckness for a while until the associated anxiety subsides. I'm not talking about habitual or high-level anxiety that is recurrently experienced (in which case professional assistance is indicated rather than doing nothing and waiting it out), I'm talking about something that feels more like a frustrating yearning for a familiar experience of quiet-mind that for some reason feels out of reach.

In such a case, doing nothing and not writing (or speaking) about it for a short while can help create the ease of mind that allows intuition to present options. Sometimes I get stuck, not because there is an absence of ideas, but because my mind is too full or too attentive to a particular, probably logical, outcome. If there is an urgency dictated by a deadline, it can be difficult to trust that standing still is a constructive method of addressing the situation.

However, in my experience, the time it takes to be quiet and attentively restful yields more progress than the actions that come out of my anxious-mind. If I can't write, I know it is an indication to step away from writing; and the same goes for sitting in meditation.

Ask Questions

When feeling stuck, especially if you are willing to move but don't know what is the appropriate choice of direction, I recommend introducing questions in your meditation practice. I don't address the question to anyone or anything in particular; I simply introduce to my mind a question and sit with it.

Sometimes I have to wait it out while my mind brainstorms possible answers. I have to wait until all that fast thinking simmers down so that I can sit with the unanswered question. I do this because I have noticed that making acquaintance with the question has the effect of tuning me in to possible answers, even if I encounter those answers later in the week. With the question in my mind, I'm more likely to notice a song on the radio, for example, and connect its relevance to the matter at hand than if I am dwelling on how to solve my problem.

Questions could be "What is the best possible outcome in this situation?" "What do I need to let go of in order for movement to take place in this situation?"

"Where do I need to become bigger, wiser, or stronger in this situation?" "What is the next step for me to take in this situation?"

I write a question such as the ones above at the top of a blank page or journal. Then I sit in meditation with eyes closed, from time to time opening them to read the question, but delay writing anything else on the page until my sitting time is complete. Sometimes I return to my written answers years later, and I have found them to be an inspiration to read, both as a history of my growth and as an inspiration to further development.

Go Back to Basics

When feeling stuck, especially if the stuckness is typified by feelings of being overwhelmed, simplify your practice and go back to short, easy meditations. You might sit for only ten minutes in unstructured quietness, or if you don't typically listen to music during your sitting practice, you might put on some music and listen to it. This is a good time to walk in nature without thought as to being mindful or present; even a walk in nature with an occupied mind is beneficial in comparison to sticking with the feeling of stuckness.

Take a Time-Out

Sometimes you may experience a feeling of frustration and not recognize it as being stuck. If you scan your life, you may, however, notice some telltale signs such as an increase in uncharacteristic emotion or thoughts, especially of a stressful quality, and the reduction of your tolerance for disturbances. You may be expressing that negative emotion internally in the form of increased downbeat self-talk, or reversion to poor eating and sleeping habits.

Sometimes friends will notice my stuckness before I do, perhaps asking, "Is something going on with you?" If they do ask such a question and I react defensively to it, I know for sure they have spotted something happening in me that deserves attention and maybe a time-out. A time-out for me is especially effective if it includes a change in environment or doing something atypical. For example, a walk around the neighborhood if I have been indoors too much, or going to a movie, something I rarely do, can help rebalance things very nicely.

Read

Another suggestion to help move through a time of stuckness is to use spiritual readings. If you find yourself in a spiritual desert, it may be time to read instead of meditating or journaling. You may read something spiritual and uplifting, but if you have no taste for that, it may be time for you to read a science fiction novel or another genre that you love and haven't read for a long time. It's very helpful if you find yourself in a spiritual no-movement zone and it seems impossible for you to sit still, or generate words in a journal, or feel anything at all. What I do sometimes is focus on a peaceful reading, or a good novel, or favorite poetry.

Take Shelter in the Company of Other Meditators

Practicing alone has its benefits in that you can tailor your practice to your preferences. There is, however, something powerful that takes place in a group of people meditating together. When feelings of stuckness prevent me from committing to my practice, I find that joining an established group of meditators is helpful for a while and can often jump-start me. It is not uncommon to find meditation groups in local spiritual communities that will allow drop-in or short-term attendance. I like taking shelter in groups of other meditators because there is something about the established momentum in the room that draws me in, and on occasion it has been like hitching a ride until I was refreshed enough to travel by my own power.

Take Heart, It Happens

In a beautifully practical guide to learning how to pray, Helene Ciaravino offers this comfort to those who encounter spiritual low spots:

> Don't let your spiritual "lows" scare you; they are worth every effort it takes to overcome them. As you advance in your prayer life, you will be developing a more mature relationship with God, and along with this growth might come growing pains. During tough times, remind yourself that unanswered prayers and spiritual dry spells are opportunities, not death sentences. They have the power to deepen your understanding of prayer. Such hurdles strengthen your prayer muscle, teaching you to look beyond simple "yes" answers and feel-good prayers, into a more profound spiritual life.*

* Helene Ciaravino, *How to Pray: Tapping into the Power of Divine Communication* (Garden City Park, NY: Square One Publishers, 2001), p. 217.

TRY THIS

Journaling as a Meditative Practice

Get a blank journal or notepad and resolve to use it for this meditative assignment only. Select a time and place where you can spend uninterrupted time with your notebook every day for seven days. Modify these directions to meet your schedule needs, aiming to spend time writing daily, preferably at the same time every day. Using a timer, allow for fifteen minutes of uninterrupted writing.

Write about anything. If you get stuck, write about what you did the previous day, or about a recent movie, or describe your last meal, or recount a conversation you've had. When the timer announces the fifteen-minute mark, set down your pen and go back to the beginning of your writing to read through in a slow, unhurried manner.

Do not attempt to analyze or read meaning into the text, just read it in a quiet, unhurried pace.

Appreciation as a Meditative Practice

Another exercise you can practice with a journal or notepad during your scheduled meditation practice time, or last thing in the evening before bed, is to write a daily list of people, experiences, creatures, or objects you are grateful for. Or you can carry a notebook around with you in a pocket and make a game of it. The idea is to look for small things around you to be grateful for, to begin to notice the things in life that are easily taken for granted. When I do this practice, I start with the physical objects closest to me. I write on the top of the page "I am grateful for . . ." and then start listing the things: my clothing, the chair I'm sitting on, and so forth. The next day I start all over with a new list on a new page, and to my surprise, there are infinite layers of objects in my world that I can acknowledge.

Thank-You Cards

Give yourself a whole week to enjoy this practice. You'll need at least seven thank-you cards, envelopes and stamps, and a notebook. The notebook can be used to keep track of everything anyone does for you or gives to you. For example, a co-worker brings your printout from the printer to your desk, or a neighbor brings your garbage can in, or a checkout clerk remembers you. Then, once a day each day during the week that you have decided to do this exercise, make a commitment to write at least one thank-you note. Make it short and simple. Don't get bogged down by perfectionism or concerns about producing just the right tone. Don't do it via e-mail. Don't send a text message. Send a handwritten short note or card with a simple expression of gratitude. The results of this week's practice should be delightful and amazing to you and your targeted recipients. If it is an employee in a store that you notice, writing a note to their supervisor and/or company is as effective, since you don't know the individual's personal information.

KEYS:

1. Abandon the idea that you can make your thinking do something.

2. Be willing for one week to daily write down your thoughts to provide a way for you to examine what is in them.

Food for Thought—Pratipaksha Bhavanam

In the Yoga Sutras of Patanjali, there is mention of a practice called "Pratipaksha Bhavanam," which is an effective way of redirecting and slowing down hurried thoughts, especially if those thoughts are disturbing or painful. My understanding of the practice is that it consists of identifying stressful thoughts and purposefully forming the exact opposite thought in mind. To me the practice came to life when I began writing my thoughts down in an unhurried and unedited way. Without the slowdown of writing, it was practically impossible to perform the action of forming exact opposite thoughts in the mind. Sometimes when writing, I would notice disturbing ideas, fearful trends in

151

the words. When this happened, I would do an exercise inspired by my understanding of Pratipaksha Bhavanam. On a separate page I would try writing down the opposite of each disturbing thought as a way of "trying on" an alternative perspective. Sometimes the result would prompt laughter, other times it would feel contrived, and yet at other times the practice would nudge out into the open a perspective I hadn't considered. If I noticed in my journal writing a phrase such as "I am too old," I would write the opposite on a separate page, "I am too young." Just sitting with the new phrase would sometimes bring relief if the original thought had been painful or challenging.

The practice has been helpful when sitting in meditation and a disturbing thought arises. I don't try to change the disturbing thought; instead, I call to mind a situation in which the opposite emotions and experience took place. If I cannot think of an actual experience, then I try to imagine one that is the opposite. This practice requires willingness to use your imagination and benefits from playfulness. It isn't an attempt to manipulate or negate the validity of painful experiences; it is instead a way of relieving pressure and pain through a shift in perspective. For example, if I discover myself fixatedly rethinking a challenging communication and carefully planning out the response, I pause and try to think about and meticulously look for a different time when a communication I had was pleasant and inspiring. I know I still have to deal with the difficult communication; it doesn't go away on account of this exercise in shifting perspective. But what can and sometimes does go away is the obsessive energy, and with it the need to retaliate. The phrase "Pratipaksha Bhavanam" means to contemplate or meditate on the opposite and is meant to be applied to turbulent and disturbing thoughts. The more disturbing the thought being addressed, the more challenging the practice. Sometimes shifting location can contribute to shifting mental energy; for example, if in your usual meditation time, in your usual spot, you seem not to be able to escape disturbing thoughts, then getting up and going outside or to nature can be helpful. Instead of trying to think of an actual opposite to whatever is disturbing you, thinking instead of something in nature, like a lake or tree or stone, particularly if you're looking at it, can help create the spaciousness in thought.

9

ENGAGING WITH YOUR SELF

> O Krishna, the stillness of divine union which you
> describe is beyond my comprehension. How can
> the mind, which is so restless, attain lasting peace?
> Krishna, the mind is restless, turbulent, powerful,
> violent; trying to control it is like trying to tame
> the wind.
>
> BHAGAVAD GITA 6:33–34

Leave Me Alone

Meditation is something you do with your self, which is
exactly what makes it challenging for some people. One of
the recurring concerns among people I teach or counsel
spiritually is their discomfort with being alone. Yet, it is my
experience that when we can contentedly be alone without

distraction, we can get a clear sense of our place in the scheme of things and we can expect confidence and self-esteem to increase.

Some people have their identity wrapped up in their partner, their career, or family, so much so that they have forgotten who they are without those identifiers, and silence—the experience in which they would reflect on their identity—is not strongly embraced in our culture.

The opposite seems to be the case in our society. Every moment is jammed full with data, sounds, and experience. I have a friend who leaves his radio on all the time in the background at a very low level while he is driving. The sound is too low to distinguish what is being broadcast, but without the background noise, he feels disconcerted and edgy. I have the opposite experience, and when he drives me somewhere I begin to feel uneasy because on the periphery of my consciousness is this low-level sound that I can't properly decipher. The background sound distracts me from being present.

Another friend cannot sleep unless the television is playing all night. Many people are simply uncomfortable with silence, whether that is in a lull in conversation or in a too quiet atmosphere in a restaurant or at a party. Silence for some almost conveys a message that something is out of place.

Being constantly subject to sounds and information, a person is left with little other option than to attempt to integrate it and sort out what is useful and what is not, and this takes up almost all of their available time and energy. As a result, little to no time is spent communing with the internal world and its peace.

Without the balancing action of time spent alone in inner silence, separated from the stimuli of the world around us, it is difficult to maintain a confident sense of self. Constant exposure to people, noises, information can, if sustained without pause, contribute to behavior that is called being "burned out." When you know how to—and frequently do—access alone time, you take advantage of an inner world in which your mental analysis and even your opinions and ideas can take a rest.

In that interior world of silent nurturing peace, I like to say, is where we encounter ourselves in the form of our undisturbed, innocent self. In other words, there is a frame of mind in which you are balanced, unpressured, not manipulated, and that frame of mind is available primarily, it seems, when you are alone in quietness. It is for that state of mind, primarily, that I meditate.

Creating time to be alone may require some creativity and commitment to rescheduling. The best-case scenario is that you will be able to create time in your life to be utterly alone in an undisturbed environment such as in nature at the ocean, or in your home. If it is wholly impossible to create such a scheduled alone time right away, you might consider joining groups that practice silent meditations until either your schedule eases up or you become comfortable enough embracing being left alone with your quiet self.

If you are able to schedule time to be alone, and if being alone is new to you, you may not want to launch into extended silent meditation right away. You might experiment with activities, selected for their potential to increase mindful awareness, and to increase purposefully paying attention to what is happening. For example, smelling, peeling, and eating an apple in an unhurried and mindful way can be an exercise in staying gently attentive to what you are doing. In this way, you are not losing yourself, indeed more of yourself is being present for the activity. Adopting an attitude of patience helps you stay with the small actions associated with eating the apple, and without rushing to the end result, each motion can and does expose a world of sensory beauty.

As a musician, I find that playing an instrument has an interesting meditative quality that transports me to a peaceful, focused place. Although not exactly alone with myself, I am deeply and profoundly unified with the musical experience and the instrument.

Ten Minutes of Sanctuary

In a class about spiritual living, I began each week's session with a short ten minutes of silence, as much for my own presence of mind as for the contribution it made to the students' peace. In the final class during the break, I asked a student what had been most helpful for him in the class we were about to complete. "The half hour we sit in silence at the beginning of class," he responded sincerely. "At first I found it impossible to sit still, and almost felt frightened by the degree of agitation I felt and thought I'd never get through it. But because everyone else seemed OK, I decided to stick with it and as soon as I made that decision, I found the silence was like a vacation from the world and I've come to really enjoy it."

I explained to him that it was only ten minutes silence, leaving him disbelieving. He had not referenced his watch and had imagined the time in quiet to be much longer than it was in actual minutes. We got to talk about how he might do the same thing at home alone with the assistance of a timer.

Later, when I checked with him, he reported that it hadn't been as easy, and that there was something about being with the group that created the comfort zone that allowed him to give way to the practice. In addition, he found it helpful to know that someone else would be keeping track of the time and signal when it was time to continue with regular class activities.

Even though he quoted the silent meditation in class as the most helpful of all the material presented, he seemed unwilling to establish it as a practice for himself. I was very interested in this and without any accusation asked him if he could explain his decision to me a little more. In a heartwarming conversation, he disclosed to me that he was afraid of being alone with himself, and had a core belief that if he looked too closely within himself, he would discover something that was so radically broken that he wouldn't know what to do about it. He shared that this idea of his original brokenness came from repeated conditioning in his religion of origin, and that although he was attracted to the idea of a quiet-mind, and also to the thought that there was something serene and wholesome within him, he had difficulty in making the transition from one worldview about humanity to another.

This student, and others like him, benefit from taking things very slowly at first. In these cases I recommend beginning with the academic study of meditation, by reading how-to manuals as well as studies about the benefits of meditation to build a foundation of trust and comfort, while at the same time experimenting with easy, but regular, stretches of time in unstructured quietness.

Taking time to be alone is not intended to displace our social interactions, which are very important to healthy living. Rather, the alone time contributes to our ability to interact and engage in mutual support and will likely improve our ability to listen and communicate well. In our alone time, we access the quiet that gives us support during periods of stress, tragedy, and suffering; however, social interactions cannot be underestimated for providing similar nurturance and support.

Meditation is not the pathway to withdrawal from society. It does, however, provide a retreat from society for the purpose of shoring up inner resources and arriving at clarity about boundaries and choices. Our practice is to become more at ease with the beautiful quietness that is already within us, and to become more at ease with the process of being alone so that we can access that quietness. It is not intended to replace community or renounce life and its splendidness; instead, it is a pathway to reducing alienation, fear, and worry.

We can accomplish this by creating a retreat from the regular pace and activities of our world. It doesn't need to be on a mountaintop or in an exotic location, although these are wonderful, too. It may very well be that your own home can be a suitable place for retreat, even if you share it with others. With just a little creativity and some agreements, you can make some space to be alone and undisturbed. In a house that is home to many occupants, the agreement to designate a specific space to have undisturbed access by one person for a period of time for the purpose of extended silent meditation is an agreement that affects everyone.

We had a group of visiting monks set up and create a colored sand mandala as part of a demonstration of their particular spiritual and meditative practices. What I remember most of all about the event are two incidents, the first being that an enthusiastic and curious toddler fell over and into the more than half-completed sand mandala. I remember it because of the pleasant and unflustered way in which the monks smiled, adjusted and repaired it. It reminded me to have broad-minded lenience about life when it does impinge upon my calmness and well-laid plans for creating serenity and sanctuary.

The other incident I remember is that of the head monk

taking time daily to retreat into a room that we agreed to make available to him for long periods of undisturbed time. It affected everyone in the building. Not only was the head monk unavailable for consultation and not present at meals, but additionally there was a palpable feeling of mindfulness in the building as we went about our regular business with just that much more tranquility, as if our quietness was contributing to his retreat.

Whether we have the luxury of taking extended time off, or whole days at a time weekly, or if our practice is a modest ten minutes of silence once a week in a group, the idea is that when we know our way there, we will likely want more of it; and when we avail ourselves of its nurturing silence, a change takes place in us so that, when we return to our normal life activities, we are no longer at the mercy of the type of mind that Prince Arjuna in the Bhagavad Gita is concerned by—"restless, turbulent, powerful, and violent." And yet though the world around us continues to be shaped and disturbed by events that have their origin in minds that are so troubled, some part of the quiet we practice will linger with us as we walk through our responsibilities, and in this way I believe we make a beneficial contribution to the world.

Sanctuary Your Way

Some students in my meditation class shared that sitting quietly indoors presented them with an impossible block to overcome. They related to me that unless they were outside, in a garden or somewhere in nature, they simply couldn't do it. They couldn't overcome the feeling of being restricted and cut off from life when sitting indoors, no matter how mindfully they prepared the place where they were to sit.

Something beautiful, expansive, even calming happens, they would report, when outside, whether sitting on a park bench or walking in a quiet neighborhood. The air and sky seem to have a powerful effect on our well-being regardless of whether we have found our perfect meditation practice or not.

So I encouraged students to declare that time spent outdoors was a legitimate meditation practice and to begin to report their findings by keeping notes in a journal after each time they spent in quiet outdoors. They did, and important details began to emerge, among them being that there seems to be a fine line between a pleasant outdoor activity and a meditation experience that leads to a quiet mind.

163

Key is the amount of stimulation created by the mental attention required for the activity, and whether or not that degree of focus on the activity interferes with being able to observe your mind without effort. Another key is the intentionality with which one engages in the outdoor activity.

For example, if I go to nature with the intention of courting a quiet-mind, that intention informs my decisions about where to go, and whether or not it is appropriate to the exercise to take someone along with me, and so on. Outdoors at a busy beach with friends on a summer day may yield a different experience to time spent outdoors alone on a bench near a pond.

One student reported that for him, walking the dog outdoors could not be properly substituted for meditation because of the amount of care and attention his enthusiastic dog demanded from him. The dog's joyful exuberance proved far too engaging, and every tree, person, and passing canine became a festival of happiness, Walking the dog for him was a necessary and enjoyable recreation activity and once he was able to identify the difference between that and activities that lead to quiet-mind, he began to make space for both time outside alone and time outside with his best friend.

I became aware of an important question that I believe each person has to ask themselves: "What detracts from my being mindfully aware of my inner life, and what contributes to being mindfully aware of my inner life?"

Whether outdoors or indoors, I began to notice the difference between being stimulated to thought versus being calmed into states I was identifying as "meditative." As I became familiar with the difference between being stimulated and calmed, I experimented by removing stimuli from my practice. I stopped playing music in the background while sitting in meditation because I noticed that for my musician's brain, music caused me to engage a good portion of my mind with analyzing the music. For others, music transports them away from their analyzing mind and toward stillness.

If I go walking in nature, I learned, I have to do it alone and not with company—that is, if I am interested in accessing a quite state of mind. I have learned that I am easily stimulated by the people and things I love, as well as by countless ordinary events and everyday things. In this regard I'm not much different from my student's puppy who loves everything she encounters when on a walk. If I do want to walk meditatively outdoors with a companion, and if my walking companion is agreeable and we share the intention of courting quiet-mind, it can change the tone of the walk and our wordless walk experience can be beautiful and profoundly peaceful.

That being said, it is very difficult, in my opinion, for me to duplicate what sitting in stillness produces with an activity such as running, exercising, dancing, or walking. When an activity requires attention to detail, such as stepping on the sidewalk, navigating the path through the woods at a running pace, synchronizing with the music, and so on, some small part of awareness is invested in that activity. Then again, I cannot deny the powerful moments experienced during the "zoning out" that takes place when I achieve a rhythm running around the lake or when I "bliss out" dancing around my house with my favorite music on (I confess, I do it).

Intentional Time Off

A friend related an exercise to me that has helped me increase my understanding of what quiet-mind feels like. In the exercise he was asked to go, from sunrise to sunset, without engaging in any activities of any kind, to the best of his ability, other than those necessitated by biology. He was not to read anything to pass the time, not to watch any

TV, not to do any writing, not to read his e-mail or any printed material, including the preparation directions or listed ingredients on products. He was free to prepare and consume meals and move about the house, but to avoid becoming engaged in tasks or activities such as tidying up anything more than the dishes he used for his meals.

I tried it for myself. I planned my next day off with the intention to have it be a day without engagement. I didn't know all the details of the exercise so I made up my own guidelines and decided I would not read, write, or otherwise engage with other people. I would spend the day alone and do only that which did not require reading, writing, and speaking.

Right from the start of my day I noticed I wanted to glance at the clock more frequently than usual. Time seemed to be dragging, which I confirmed to be an accurate assessment when I eventually did glance inadvertently at a clock—I was surprised how very little time had passed. Perhaps, I thought, it was because I was just sitting around and beginning to feel anxious that I was wasting time being unproductive. So I set about doing the laundry, but agreed with myself that I would do it mindfully and maintain the peaceful demeanor I had intended to cultivate. I already love doing the laundry, but that day was quite different. I clearly had, in this slowed-down pace, an outrageous and luxurious amount of time to dedicate to staring at the agitator frothing up the suds. I saw things I had not noticed before, patterns in the swirling water, dirt in places on the washing machine that had escaped cleaning. It reminded me of the time my car broke down and I walked to work along a route I had traveled by car for years. Walking, I saw the neighborhood as if for the first time, and it was wonderful to realize that all this rich detail had been present and available to me all the while I was hurriedly getting to the office.

Granted, not everyone can take the luxury of a whole day free of all engagements. Parents raising young children may find it difficult to set aside even thirty minutes to catch their breath. One student, a mother who had been an avid meditator, related to me that while raising her toddler, she had to plan to sit and be still during her daughter's naptime. When her second child came along, she had more to attend to and intended to meditate before going to bed. Needless to say she discovered that what she most needed then was to sleep. She related that the only place she could find to be peaceful for that year was in the bathroom, so she would practice slowing down, breathing evenly, and completing her ablutions with as little speed and as mindfully as she could until her parenting responsibilities would allow her to expand her practice more.

Doing the laundry on my day without engagement, I noticed that my measured pace encouraged a sustained attitude of quietness and satisfaction. I had none of my usual arguments about why I shouldn't have to fold T-shirts, the mystery of missing socks, or wrestling with gigantic fitted sheets that defy symmetry in folding. I resolutely performed one task after the other. From time to time I became aware that I had passed through seemingly long gaps of uncontrived quiet-mind time. I would dip in and out like a water skimmer landing briefly on the surface of a pond. The once draggingly slow pace of time somehow appeared to have zoomed quickly forward, and I found myself in the bathroom ready to brush my teeth for bed.

I ached to check my schedule, to turn on my computer so my e-mail would be ready for reading in the morning, and when I noticed this tug, I noticed also the significant shift in my mood and temperament when considering these deviations from my plan. I smiled and went to bed.

TRY THIS

Electronic Communications

Take time this week to review your electronic communications.

- *Do you check your e-mail first thing in the morning?*
- *Do you receive notifications of e-mail as they arrive and respond to text messages immediately?*
- *Do you expect to respond to communications right away?*

Make whatever modifications are possible to create more electronic-communications–free space in your day for the next seven days. For example, consider placing your smartphone far away from you in another room while you sleep. Determine a time in the day when you will begin responding to electronic communications and consider limiting the amount of time you devote to e-mail. Try responding to electronic communications on a schedule, for example, from ten a.m. to eleven thirty a.m. every second day, but no more than that. Even students who rely heavily on e-mail for business purposes have reported a significant shift in inner peace and calm by making a small shift in how available they are for e-mail responses.

Experiment with setting your e-mail provider to deliver your e-mail messages every two hours, rather than instantly.

Resolve to respond to messages no more than one or one and a half hours per day.

Ambient Sounds

Alternatively, take time this week to review background noises in your life.

- *Is your e-mail service set to make an audible sound, alerting you when an e-mail has arrived? Can you turn it off?*
- *Do you turn on the radio immediately when you get into your car? Try driving in silence.*
- *Do you turn on a radio, stereo, or television when you get home? Consider a week of no television as an experiment.*
- *What electronic devices are left running in your home, and when you sit quietly next to*

them, can you hear them? (You may discover that what you thought to be a quiet environment has many sounds generated by electrical devices. I was surprised to notice after sitting quietly each day at the same time that my home was alive with what might be considered insignificant sounds. I discovered a lamp that generated a very quiet buzz and an appliance that did the same. As I sat quietly, these noises began to take on greater prominence in my awareness and I had to take measures to quiet them, or relocate my sitting practice.)

Try to eliminate background sounds and ambient noises in your life for one week as an experiment.

Wake Up to Your Breathing

Sitting and observing your breathing is a tranquil exercise that can open up your awareness to the miracle of your body. Try noticing the difference between the qualities of the breath as it is inhaled and when it is exhaled; it is a good mindfulness practice that can support you in noticing and increasing appreciation for your body and the miracle of its ability to breathe, and for the air around us. It can also awaken appreciation for subtle differences that are every-where present, such as in the difference between inhaled and exhaled breath, but which easily go un-noticed.

I was first introduced to watching breathing as a meditation when I began studying yoga. I was invited to breathe through my nose and to pay attention to the motion of the air as it passed in and out of my body by focusing on the sensation of the air around my nostrils. I had not paid such fine-tuned attention to my breathing before and was surprised to dis-cover how much variation existed in the characteristic of air on the way in as compared to that of the air on the way out.

I began to notice that I could feel the sensation of the moving air in different places: on the way in, I sensed motion on the outer rim of my nostril, and on the way out I had more sense of the air inside my nose. Additionally, the quality of the air, I noticed, changed in each direction. On the way in, air tended to be drier. On the way out, it was both warmer and moister. I could also sometimes imagine that I was aware of the sound of the air moving.

Later, in another class, I was invited to count my breaths. One inhalation-exhalation pair was to be one count. The idea was to determine how many pairs I could stay aware for and count. Try it yourself. Generally, people report after the exercise that their attention would wander after a fairly short period of counting. The instruction is to gently return to counting, starting again at one so as to have a way to measure how long you can stay with the practice of watching your breath.

Perhaps because of my yoga instruction, I found the exercise to be pleasingly engaging, yet I would still lose track of the counting. It made me appreciate the value and function of having counting devices such as beads or beans when engaging in an exercise that was prescribed to go on for a specific count.

KEYS:

1. Reduced environmental stimulation can enhance your meditation practice.

2. Reduced electronic stimulation and communication responsibilities can enhance your meditation practice.

Food for Thought—It's More Than Relaxation Time

Meditation, although relaxing, is not merely a relaxation technique. If I'm not relaxed and calm, it's pretty much impossible for me to meditate until I am relaxed and calm. So now, I run to relax before I meditate so that when I meditate I'm open to the deeper experience. In *Calming Your Anxious Mind*, Dr. Jeffrey Brantley lists six thoughts about what meditation is not. The second thought, and the one that relates to this chapter's focus, is, "Meditation is not just another relaxation technique." Although relaxation and recreation are important parts of a balanced life, they are different activities and have different effects on meditation. Dr. Brantley writes that meditation *seeks in-*

creased awareness, and that awareness brings wisdom and freedom from habitual reactions. Similarly, meditation is not the same as positive thinking, or going into an altered state of mind. It can instead be thought of as the practice of purposefully paying attention to thoughts. Rather than a technique for escaping reality, it is a practice of being available for reality and staying present for whatever is current. Meditation is not a way of avoiding responsibilities, duties, and agreements. It is a practice that leads to responding to our life with resiliency and accountability.

I particularly appreciate Dr. Brantley's reminder that the practice of meditation is not to be thought of as something belonging to monks or spiritual practitioners. It is relearning something that is innate in us—the capacity to be conscious of what is going on around us and in us. It isn't a special talent reserved for a certain few, or something that belongs to practitioners of certain faith traditions. It is for everyone, and everyone has a way of approaching meditation that matches them. Then again, some people who take purposeful time to practice being present report a shift in awareness that feels quite different from ordinary awareness. Some might even describe the shift as an altered state of mind, but not in the sense of reality being altered or distorted, but in the sense of an increased noticing of details, colors, shapes, surfaces, and the like.

Ideally, Thich Nhat Hanh* writes, we should spend every day and every hour practicing being mindful, but in reality we have obligations and agreements that put such a goal out of reach for many people. So, he recommends, we ought to reserve one day a week to devote entirely to practice. A day like a Sabbath, a day without planned engagement, to be set aside to focus on focusing, to be aware of awareness, a day of mindfulness, which you select and consider a date with yourself. First moments in the morning of your day of mindfulness are critical, and if you can devise some way to immediately remind yourself in your waking moments that *today is my day of mindfulness practice*, you will notice a substantial increase in the deepness of the experience, in comparison to gradually remembering that today is the day you were to practice. Thich Nhat Hanh recommends hanging something in a place that you are likely to look at immediately upon awakening, for example, a sign with the word "Mindfulness" on it so that you will instantly be invited into practice mode. That way, whatever your first steps of the morning are, you can perform them with all due carefulness and calmness. Over time, a single day of mindfulness during a week begins to have impact on the days surrounding it. Looking forward

* Thich Nhat Hanh. *The Miracle of Mindfulness, A Manual on Meditation* (Boston: Beacon Press, 1987), p. 27.

to it, you might notice yourself beginning to enter the mindset of mindfulness the day before. The day after, you may find some of the calmness lingering in your activities. Thich Nhat Hanh writes that:

> *The day of mindfulness will begin to penetrate the other days of the week, enabling you to eventually live seven days a week in mindfulness.** *

* Thich Nhat Hanh, *The Miracle of Mindfulness*, p. 31.

10

DISCOVERING A NEW SPIRITUALITY

Just remember that I am, and that I support the entire cosmos with only a fragment of my being.

BHAGAVAD GITA 10:42

Think on These Things

At some point, meditation helped me begin to undo the stitching that held together the theology that had been trained into me in my formative years. The core of it was that there is something essentially wrong with humans and that the only path out of that damaged state was to compensate with sustained regret and an attempt to behave in a good way despite the intrinsic wrongness I was born with.

Sitting and watching my thinking while in meditation, I crossed a line into a new world of spirituality, and instead of seeing human life's flaws as something to despise, I started to develop a genuine love of life's eccentricities, seeing them less and less as intrinsic flaws. I began to appreciate my own fear of impermanence, my own tendencies to self-preservation and competition, not as qualities to hate but as potentials shared with all beings. I began to see my life as one of simply endless ways of expressing. I began to hold less fiercely the grudges I had against people who seemed not to be able to refrain from unkind actions when I saw the numerous instances in which I was incapable of doing what I insisted they do.

I say that I began to fall in love with people. I can't say that I am never distressed by other people's choices or that circumstances in life never stress me out, but I don't judge my less beautiful responses to life as being evidence of my essential brokenness. I can't say I understand all of humanity, and what makes a person lie, steal, and murder remains an unsolved mystery to me.

However, the saying "There is a bit of larceny in every person's heart" became something I kept close as I became increasingly aware that everything exists as a potential for all beings—such is the nature of freedom—and the saying reminds me, when thinking of tragedies and violence, to look also for the aggressor in me and where the potential for aggression remains. I discovered a new spirituality in the form of an assignment to prove my own beliefs by how I show up in the world. And meditation has helped me stay on task with that assignment.

Now, when I sit in stillness, I am accustomed to finding what potentials exist within me and notice which destructive tendencies have taken up residence inside. Not to evict them, or to declare war on them, but to see them as part of the vast and colorfully complicated nature of inner life, and to accept my assignment of choosing the most honorable way to live.

Distressed and Preoccupied

In pursuit of this new spirituality, and in the process of wrestling with what tendencies I discovered in me, there were times when I couldn't find the peace of the witness within and there were times in which I came to my meditation practice distressed and preoccupied. The row going on in my head rang alarms of danger and forced my body into high-alert status and readiness to flee. In such times, a half hour of sitting felt like a week in a torture chamber, I imagined. There were times I had to employ strategies to address the state of restlessness that would not abate through sitting. One such strategy I remembered from my early childhood when I learned to recite the Rosary and gained much comfort from doing so.

At my young age, I didn't perfectly understand the meaning of the words I was reciting, yet that did not diminish the effect of bringing peace and comfort through the rhythmic repetition of words, and by keeping track of them with counting beads. The activity displaced my preoccupations, and looking back now, I recognize the state of mind I achieved after the repetitions as the same quiet-mind I encounter today through meditation.

As an adult, I lost contact with the practice and remembered it again when visiting India, where I observed a similar practice of reciting prayers or significant phrases a hundred and eight times, keeping track of the recitation with *mala*, or prayer beads. I purchased my own set of beads as soon as I could, and printed out one of the world's most ancient prayers, the Gayatri Mantra:

> *Om bhur bhuvah suvah*
> *tat savitur varen yam*
> *bhargo devasya dhīmahi*
> *dhiyo yó nah pracodayāt*

Swami Vivekananda offers a free-form translation of the ancient prayer to be:

*We meditate on the glory of that Being who has produced this universe; may He enlighten our minds.**

I started reciting and counting. I didn't mind so much that I only knew an approximation of what each word in the ancient prayer means, because something about the ancientness of the words and the image of endless generations of people reciting it conveyed something comforting and powerful to me. I was looking for and had found an activity that would occupy my troubled mind.

It took me awhile to find my rhythm like I had with the rosary. I remember when I first introduced this meditation practice to a group I was leading in Bali, that those not familiar with the practice wondered if they would be able to last through what they estimated would surely take a very long time to complete.

In practice, the hundred and eight recitations take about twenty-five minutes to complete, and when done, especially when a group completes them, the attending silence is not only internal but also present in the room as a palpable stillness. Oftentimes, after this meditative practice, participants appear to be reluctant to leave the room.

....

* *The Complete Works of Swami Vivekanand* (Advaita Ashram, India, 1915), p. 211.

Some students have related to me their sincere desire to use this method, but encounter a significant block in the form of the foreign text. In some cases, the unknown words resulted in a feeling of disconnection to the process; in other cases, there was a concern that the sentiment expressed in the prayer was not entirely in sync with their religious beliefs. We have discussed options, including selecting a prayer or sayings that can be substituted—something that when recited can be committed to memory, in other words, not too long, and not too short. Something in which all the words and all the meaning are agreeable to the one reciting them.

Alternate versions, paraphrases, or free-form translations of well-known prayers have met the need for some, like this prayer I wrote inspired by the Lord's Prayer:

Infinite Presence within,
Your nature is wholeness and perfection.
You are eternally present everywhere.
And from within You guide me.
For Your ways are my ways.
Infinite Power within,
my every need is contained within You.
As I dwell on Your nature,
I am released from all previous errors.

And I am able to release the errors of others.
With my mind centered on You,
I am empowered to be all that I can be today,
a worthy channel for good.
I am strong and courageous,
through the Power and to the glory of God which is Love
Amen.

Or personally selected phrases that are meaningful:

Within me is joy everlasting
Within me is love ever growing
Within me is peace, peace, peace.

Or a few lines, for example, from a favorite song, such as Michael Gott's "I Will Make a Quiet Place":

I will make a quiet place,
A quiet place within my life,
And I will wait upon the Lord,
Wait upon the Lord.

Everywhere Present

My journey with meditation began as a quest to live a more spiritual life than the one I was living. According to my understanding at the time, there was "spiritual living," and there was everything else. I very much wanted to make the evolutionary move from the "everything else" category to that of "spiritual person." I had been raised thinking about life in these terms of polar opposites: human nature on one side and God-nature on the other, with a chasm between the two not necessarily intended to be crossed. It wasn't any surprise to me when I first began sitting, writing, and watching my thoughts that I discovered dark, mean-spirited opinions living inside my mind. The discovery seemed to confirm what I had been raised to expect of humans—that we were intrinsically flawed and must work diligently to overcome our original nature. I think the spiritual life I was aiming for was, at best, a form of stifling undesirable feelings and managing detrimental inclinations. The goal was to show up well in the world despite the tangled web of unkindness lurking beneath the surface on the inside.

It was through reading the Bhagavad Gita that I again encountered a new spirituality in the form of the idea of something that is everywhere present, connecting all of everything. God, for want of a better term, seemed an appropriate word to use to describe that something, although I by no means mean to refer to the supernatural being of my childhood religious training. I was beginning to think something that was new to me, an idea of something that would be everywhere present. I liked Paul Tillich's term "the ground-of-all-being" and began using the phrase interchangeably with the term "God" to describe this something that connects all of life.

My practice of sitting and observing my inner life helped me notice connections between ideas and outcomes, people, things, and thoughts. I started to think of life as being supported by some single thread that every person is somehow part of, and although not conscious of this connection, I began to realize, all have access to it. As a result of the growing awareness of my kinship with all life, I became less inclined to reject my human nature, I learned to watch it instead with compassion and to notice that underneath my less-than-charitable expressions there was some inkling of a desire to express something more loving.

Whether through conditioning or forgetfulness, I seemed to lack the skill to trust that more loving expression. Nevertheless, by being willing to patiently and regularly look within through meditation, I softened in my assessment of good-bad when I could, shifting to a more neutral assessment of my thoughts. I began to witness my thoughts like guests at a family gathering, some rowdy, others not, some polite, others not. But all of them part of me.

I learned to be increasingly more gracious with these parts of myself, even though there were some I could barely countenance and regretted to admit were part of the inner family. Over time, I began to notice that my rowdy thoughts were similar to those also present in other people, and that they struggled also to trust their inclination to unite, love, and share. I noticed more and more connections and similarities between people. Then I began to notice how a little bit of everyone and everything could be found everywhere at all times.

Universal, Permanent, Eternal, Uncaused

The chasm I had imagined between ordinary life and spiritual life seemed to be changing, the gap was narrowing, and there were times when I think I couldn't clearly tell the difference between the two. I began to think that in order to live a "real" life—in contrast to sleepwalking through life—it would be helpful to embrace life with as much kindness and compassion as I was capable of.

Now I tend look to life as that which is everywhere present and which connects everything, and I prefer the word "Life" when talking about what I think the idea "God" might mean. Now, when I use the word "God" or encounter it in a poem, hymn, or prayer, I think of it as referring to that which is universal, permanent, eternal, uncaused, and without conditions; that which is always present. I have spent some time meditating on what these words mean to me, and experimented with definitions in the following way: Whatever it (life or God) is, if it is indeed universal, what could that mean about its nature? Whether sitting quietly with the question, or through writing it on the top of a page in a blank notebook to be followed by stream of consciousness journaling, I'd come up with something like, *It means to me that it must be equally present everywhere and in all things, not more amplified in one individual than in another. It wouldn't be a good candidate for the term "universal" if it belonged only to one culture, religion, or geographic location.*

Through this examination of my understanding of the words, I wasn't coming up with a single new idea, it had all been expressed before; yet my meditation on the term was helping me discard concepts of a regional deity with petty character insecurities. It was helping me discover something larger to dwell on, something that did not require my belief in it or obedience to it, because it was unmoved by such fluctuations in me. In other words, it is permanent, another word I meditated on to help arrive at some further clarity.

"Permanent" to me means that whatever it is, it is always in the same state regardless of experiences and history. It does not fluctuate between moods and temperaments and cannot be lost, altered, or destroyed; otherwise it would not be a good contender to the title of "permanent." Similarly, I explored the word "eternal" as a descriptor for God, and sat with the idea that whatever it is, it didn't start and doesn't end, so it is available all the time. This was a particularly helpful meditation practice, because it gave me the opportunity to compare eternal with the qualities of temporariness.

What is eternal and what is immortal? This became a fascinating lens through which to look at the world and observe how easily I could turn to things that are temporary in the hopes that they would deliver some sense of permanence and safety. Now, rather, I can love them precisely because of their impermanent and fragile nature. God as eternal would need to be beyond limits that are associated with cycles, generations, seasons, and every other kind of coming and going.

Many times during this contemplative process, I would

find myself to be idea-less and in a state of not-knowing. I see now that this was part of the journey of shedding inherited thoughts, as well as part of the process of encountering that which cannot be adequately defined with words. It had been my norm to be anxious when confronted with something I couldn't explain, and in the absence of meaning, to provide a created meaning. Through meditation, I was learning the reality of how expansive the extent of our not-knowing is, and to be more comfortable with that.

In the Beginning

I once had come upon the description of God as "First Cause," and asked myself what came before the first cause, and what would "uncaused" mean, and wouldn't "uncaused" be a fitting explanation of the nature of God? I sat silently for days and wrote pages of journal notes on what these and other absolute terms might mean, and it was gratifying to do so. Slowly unhitching myself from unsupportable ideas from a distant and ancient past about what God is or, more accurately, was, I started to refine what was becoming my new spirituality.

"Uncaused" as a term for God helped me explore the idea of no beginning, and the phrase "in the beginning" began to mean to me the beginning of any created thing, before which is the "beginninglessness" of reality. A student explained to me that it all started with a big bang, which it may very well have. And before the big bang, in whatever vastness of nothingness or everythingness that preceded the big bang, and beyond every big bang before it, is what I call God.

It's what I think about when I recite the mantra that appears at the end of the Mahāyāna Buddhist sutra known as the Heart Sutra: *"Gate gate paragate parasamgate bodhi svaha!"* I take it to mean "Gone, gone, gone beyond gone utterly beyond, Oh such an awakening!" It reminds me of the vastness of being and to go utterly beyond the forms and ideas I have become constrained by and to go beyond them by entertaining the idea of not-knowing. When I think of that God-something as vastness that is everywhere present, and consider it to be present in me and you, I begin to think about what might be already present in us regardless of our history, gender, culture, and other defining qualities.

Whatever it is in me and you, we didn't make it be there, and we cannot unmake it. Furthermore, I began to explore that you and I don't have to generate it in us, neither do we attain it, and it isn't the result of enlightenment or study and there is no becoming worthy of it, it is merely a fact of being.

Temperance and Temptation

Awareness of what it is that connects us to everything, of that which is already inside of us, is sometimes obscured by the rich diet of sensory input around us. One way to open up space to examine within is to withdraw somewhat from that rich diet from time to time, or at least temper it for a while. Temperance is not a common word in our culture today, where the focus seems to be more on gratification, in particular quick gratification. Temperance means moderation, not for the purpose of suffering or for self-punishment, but for the purpose, ultimately, of having a deeper, more lavish experience of consciousness.

A student once told me about a workshop she had attended with the title "When Enough Is Too Much." She related to me that the focus of the workshop was, in her opinion, to break the spell that has people believing that they need to possess *more than enough* to be secure and that they must hoard, collect, and attract what they need to get to that point of enoughness.

Hearing the account of this workshop touched me deeply, and although I cannot remember who taught the workshop, I can remember the title, and it evokes in me memories of difficult times in my life that turned out in the end to be moments of my greatest growth. I have adopted a practice of looking at what I have, in the midst of not having enough, with a view for identifying what is already plentiful in the midst of the lack I think I perceive.

Temperance is the voluntary restraint from excess, and I have found being aware of it has tremendous power in this culture of excess. The conscious decision to practice moderation has physical and mental benefits. Consider what too much food does to your body, too much alcohol does to your mind, too much stress does to your peace. I try to look at where I am doing something too much, and I find plenty of opportunities to apply temperance and to enjoy the benefits of doing so. Do you eat too much, self-indulge too much, and sit too much? If you can find a place where you're out of balance in this way, I propose that you will find in that place also a deficiency of abundance, possibly because you seldom venture beyond the patterns of your indulgence into the field of limitless possibilities that is characteristic of life.

I have found that through the act of voluntarily stepping back from an excess, my thought is cleared up and I become more keenly appreciative of the powerful influence that desires play in my life. It also contributes to a sense of personal accomplishment and resilience. Each time I voluntarily tone down an excess, I feel the growing strength in my awareness that I can do that. Over time it builds a case for attempting larger changes in life based on accumulated evidence that successful shifts in attitude and habit can actually happen.

I invited the members of my spiritual community one year to consider abstaining from something valuable for forty days. To put a new angle on it, I asked them to consider that if they had no daily practice of meditation, to consider giving up a life that had no meditation in it. This reverse psychology worked effectively for some who were at first strongly resistant to the idea of giving up anything at all, but who could embrace the idea that committing to forty days of daily meditation practice was a way of setting aside the time they would typically have used for something else. In this way, they believed that they were contributing to their inner life, and many reported to me afterward that the exercise changed their lives. Again, a small step that is easy to agree with is a key component for success in developing spiritual practice.

TRY THIS

Beads and a Bowl

Count out 108 beads (beans or pebbles will do too) into a bowl. Empty the bowl in front of you at the time of your scheduled meditation practice. Using a phrase or prayer of your choice, place a bean, bead, or pebble back into the bowl after each completed recitation. You could also use a prayer that you enjoy, or a poem that is uplifting, and repeat it 108 times in its entirety. If at first you cannot remember the phrase or prayer, you can refer to it on a card or in a book. If it continues to be too much for you to remember, try starting with something simpler and shorter. Another helpful memory technique is to record your own voice reciting the prayer or phrase while your eyes are open so you can see the words for all 108* recitations. Then,

....

* The word "*mala*" in Sanskrit means "garland." There are typically 108 beads on a *mala*. Traditionally the beads are held in the left hand, and with each recitation the thumb or fingers move on to the next bead. There is one central bead, sometimes larger in size, which is known as the mother or teacher bead. Generally, this bead is not intended to be used, instead, when reached (and if reciting more than 108 recitations), the direction is reversed in the beads. The number 108 is significant in many Eastern faith traditions for a variety of reasons (for example, there are 108 Upanishads in Hinduism's sacred texts, and there are 108 virtues according to some Buddhist traditions).

play back the recording for your practice so that with your eyes closed you can repeat the prayer or phrase along with your recording.

When complete, sit quietly for a few moments before continuing with the day's activities. Repeat the activity for seven days consecutively and then review your experience by writing your reflections in a journal.

God: *Then and Now*

Consider a writing assignment that describes the evolution of your understanding of the word "God" from when you were first introduced to it up until how you understand it now. If you were never introduced to the word, or if you have since abandoned the concept, consider writing about what you think the meaning might be of this phrase from the Bhagavad Gita, in which Krishna says, "Just remember that I am, and that I support the entire cosmos with only a fragment of my being." Finally, imagine you were being interviewed on prime-time television and the question posed to you is "What does the word 'God' mean to you?" Imagine answering spontaneously.

Something to Think About

During times of stress, giving the mind something to consider during meditation practice can yield peaceful results. Take a phrase that is significant to you, a positive statement about life, for example, and sit with it. Phrases I recommend include: "Forgiveness is the key to freedom," "We are one," "God is all there is," and so on. Avoid using phrases that include words that trigger you. For example, if the word "God" is one that you do not identify with or have no framework within which to relate to it, substitute it with another term that works for you (such as Life, or The Thing Itself, or The Ground of All Being, or Energy) or use an entirely different phrase to work with. Conversely, taking a phrase that includes ideas and/or words that don't resonate with you is a powerful meditation practice in itself and can lead to discovering a new way to understand your own spiritual worldview.

For example, the phrase "God is all there is" may be meaningless to you. Consider using it in the same way that you would any other phrase that has powerful meaning, in the way described below. Take a phrase and sit with it, quietly considering what it means to you. Ask yourself, "What would it mean to my life if that phrase was completely true for me? How would I show up in the world if I had complete integrity with that statement? In what way, if any, would my speaking, acting, eating, choosing be affected if that statement were a hundred percent true?" This kind of exploration can't be satisfactorily conducted with quick one-liner answers. If you grant yourself the luxury of a deeper look, you'll discover all kinds of nuances in your thinking.

KEYS:

1. When meditation is difficult because of a distressed mind, give yourself something to do, such as counting the recitations of a powerful phrase.

2. Collect inspiring phrases and quotes for your meditation practice. They will come in useful one day.

Food for Thought—Letting Go/ Letting Be

A well-known joke about faith tells the story of a man who was dangerously close to a precipice, slipped, and fell over. But as he fell, he managed to catch onto a limb of a tree growing out of the cliffside. He held tightly lest he fall to his death. When he heard footsteps somewhere above him on the ledge, he called out, "Is there anyone out there?"

A beautiful voice said, "Yes."

"Who?" yelled the dangling man.

"Why, it's God."

"Are you sure?" he inquired.

"Yes, quite sure."

"Well, help me," he yelled somewhat impatiently.

"Do you have faith?" God inquired.

"Yes."

"Do you believe I can help you?"

"Yes, yes, yes, I do."

"Then let go of the branch."

After the briefest pause, the man shouted out, "Is anyone else up there?"

This story helps me appreciate the difference between letting go and letting things be. I have been the sort of person who has needed all my *i*'s dotted and *t*'s crossed before letting go. I like it when the ducks are in a row. I have been the sort of person who likes to test the water before I dive into it. No surprises please. I would prefer a written guarantee that the water is deep enough to catch me safely, too.

But I'm finding that this is not necessarily the way of things. Life doesn't operate that way, and my hesitation while waiting for surety gets in the way of progress. I have learned to let that be—in other words, to accept the way of things. I apparently prefer to not let go without a guarantee, and life apparently doesn't work that way. I'm learning to find some peace with that realization, and I call it "letting things be as they are without fighting them."

Letting things be is not exactly the same as letting things go. Sometimes I don't want to let go of something, and I am finding that I cannot hope for substantial transformation if I work with only what is comfortable and only with what I already know or possess. If I refer too frequently to what I have accomplished in the past, it is like hanging on to the same branch, and the result is staying where I am, sometimes with diminishing fortitude.

Meditation has helped me discover if what I'm holding on to can actually hold me up. What I have found to be true more often than not is that what I think is holding me up does not have the capacity to support me the way I expect it to. I have erroneously thought of many things in my life as being the foundation upon which my life rests. Whereas there is clearly value in taking things in life quite seriously, in meditation I was able to contemplate the nature and permanence of things in a way that freed me up— not so much to let go, but to let things be what they really are. In my journaling meditation practice, I would sometimes write the phrase "I am . . ." on the top of the page and let myself complete the phrase in as many ways as I could. I have done this exercise with students in class, and in truth there is not much new on the list of things that we call upon to define ourselves: I am my relationship, I am a mother, I am a CPA, I am my sexuality, I am my gender, I am my body, and so on.

After letting these identifiers rise to the surface and sitting with them—or one at a time—investigating them so to speak, it becomes clear that each is a temporary condition, an identity that does not endure. Then the exploration of what does endure can begin. I try to keep in mind that what I am in the world (doctor, teacher, musician) and what I have in the world (job, possessions, health challenge) and what I am facing (joblessness, disappointment) is not what defines me. I try to remember that what I am doing, and the style in which I am doing it, is more likely to define me.

I've had the privilege of speaking to people as they get close to dying. Sometimes they talk about an elegant and easy process of surrendering to what is happening, and one lady told me eloquently that she was pleased to realize that the ease in the process she was experiencing seemed familiar to her because she remembered the feeling of yielding from other times in her life when she had practiced meditation and learned to give way to life. She also mentioned some regret that she had not learned to trust this natural capacity earlier in her life. She wasn't talking about the sort of trust that is a type of bargain in which we agree that if you will be good to me, then I'll be good to you. Or the kind of trust that hopes if I take care of the servicing, my car will not malfunction. She was talking about the sort of trust that requires surrender to the direction that life is going while paying attention to exactly what is happening, and finding agreement with it.

I rejected the idea of surrender when I was younger because I thought of it as giving up, and with that, images of being weak plagued me and threats of being gullible persuaded me to never surrender. Now I see that when I surrender to the direction that life is going, I am not giving up my responsibility to act in the world; I still have to make decisions and select between available options. But now these decisions and choices come out of my surrender and not out of being defeated. Sitting with the question of why I hold on so tightly sometimes, and discussing the same with people who have counseled with me, we have identified a common trait: to generate worst-case scenarios as a technique that assures a very tight hold on the present moment in which at least everything is known. "Let things be" is a phrase that has come to mean something special to me. It means to accept the moment as it is but without relinquishing the necessity to act, to choose, to investigate, to evaluate, to look for work, to balance my checkbook, to say no politely, to show up, to clean up, to 'fess up. But what is different now is the tone in which I perform these, at least in an increasing percentage of the time. Old habits die slowly and there are ample examples in my life right now where an observer reading these words, trying to match them to my behavior, would be challenged to do so.

I know why I didn't like the idea of surrender—clearly because I prefer to be able to control the outcome. Someone pointed out that our inability to control the outcome of events is a blessing in disguise, because if we were able to determine the exact outcome, then the options would be limited to only those scenarios that we could think up. That way, things might turn out to be exceedingly predictable. The observation helped me to see where in life I assume that the only options that are reasonable to take are the ones that I can think up, or have confidence in based on having experienced them already. Had I not started sitting and courting emptiness, I might have remained firm with this approach to life: hold tight. But now, in that emptiness I find a reservoir of untapped possibilities that seemingly cannot be accessed while stressful, hot thinking dominates. Meditation has helped me notice that I tend to see things according to expected patterns and has reminded me to create space in my mind for willingness to consider that there is more beyond what is presently known to me. I began to trust, or at least expect that there was "more-beyond" what I know and to embrace that unknown as part of my life. When I did counsel with people seeking insight into their spiritual lives, many would come with a familiar theme dominating their search. It goes like this: I want guidance and possibly change, and I want you to show me how to do it and to have all of the benefits while remaining exactly as I am. For some the theme presents itself as: Is there a way I can have harmonious relationships and hold on to an appropriate amount of resentment?

My experience is that these good people who seek in this way all have access to a terrific creative genius, as well as to a reservoir of untapped wisdom that is already present within us all, in the silence of our emptiness, but may not want the answer that comes from that source because it will oftentimes point in the direction of some new and unknown state of being, thinking, and behaving.

Sitting in meditation with inquiries such as "Show me the way to balance my life," "Show me the way to balance my body," "Show me how to bring my relationships into balance," "Show me how to experience abundance" is a gentle way to begin accessing the wisdom that is within. Undoubtedly what will come through in response is something like: Start an exercise program, Quit whatever, Eat this way, Start saying no to people, Take time to meditate, Begin sharing your time and resources. And sometimes we respond with:

Is there anyone else up there?
No, there isn't.
Then I think I'll just go on doing what I've always done.
After all, I've become so accustomed to the discomfort. I
don't really notice it much anymore . . .

Keep inquiring during meditation, and you'll see there is a powerful wisdom within that responds to you.

11

WHAT'S IN IT FOR ME?

> I am ever present to those who have realized me in every creature. Seeing all life as my manifestation, they are never separated from me. They worship me in the hearts of all, and all their actions proceed from me. Wherever they may live, they abide in me.
>
> BHAGAVAD GITA 6:30–31

There are definite beneficial results you can expect from practicing meditation. If you are doing your practice, you are going to see changes in how you think and feel, and in how you see your world and your place in it. It's dependable. However, you have to conduct the experiment yourself to have enduring confidence in the changes that can come about. It doesn't help to only read about it, or to only depend on the testimony of other people's inspiring changes. You've got to do your own experiment and develop a regular routine. Without the consistency of practice, the changes are going to be more difficult to experience.

When it comes to inner work, what is your daily routine? What do you do for your inner life every day? What is the ritual you perform that is as dependable as brushing your teeth?

There is not much emphasis on spiritual practice in our culture. The motto of our culture seems to be "Quicker, easier, and more convenient." It is rare that you see a popular screen actor engaged in spiritual practice as a substantial part of the story line. Indeed, if you do, the character would probably appear to be weird and out of sync with mainstream society. I was talking to a young man about the importance of having time dedicated to sitting. I discussed with him the value of carving out ten minutes a day to sit and think about something like his values. He was agreeable, yet with the same breath he asked, "Can I do it while I'm working out?"

I get that a lot when talking to people about developing a spiritual practice. *How can I make this quicker, easier, faster, and more convenient? I want what I hear is available from spiritual practice, but with the least possible inconvenience.* It could be that some people are in fact accomplished multitaskers. I know I am. I love doing many things concurrently. I have already confessed to a short span of attention when it comes to things like household chores or even creative projects, and I enjoy that in myself and when I meet it in other people. Yet, I confess that my truly lasting and profound experiences with meditation come when I give my practice of sitting focused and uncon-flicted attention. Dedicated, mindful attention is the magical ingredient in the recipe.

The word "sacred" to me means to set aside for a special purpose. When I sacrifice something, I'm not giving it up or losing it so much as I am setting it aside for a purpose that is special, or sacred. I learned to sacrifice some of my short span of attention, to give up some of my loyalty to it so that I could dedicate focused time to my practice.

When it comes to practicing meditation, different things work for different people. Things change as we change. For example, in my practice of meditation, when I first started I used to benefit from having soothing music in the back-ground. Now I don't want it, or don't need it, because it becomes just something else to listen to and dilutes the mo-ment. Yet, I can remember the deep places I went early in my practice with the assistance of music. I listened to Jon Mark's album *Land of Merlin* so many times as a back-drop to meditation that I can't hear the CD now without shifting gears, slowing down, and becoming still. So how you do it is less important than that you do it. To take the time to watch inwardly, even if only for ten minutes a day, has proven to me over and over again to be invaluable.

When you begin watching inwardly, you are going to start noticing changes. It's different for each person. Perhaps you'll notice a heightened general awareness of everything, or you'll become aware of subtle shifts in how you handle the everyday challenges that confront you. Someone described the shifts he experienced as a wheel alignment, saying his ride through life became subtly calmer and less shaky. Gratifying to him was that other people noticed the alignment in him, too.

What comes to mind are these words that are sometimes attributed to Gandhi:

Watch your thoughts, they become words;
Watch your words, they become actions;
Watch your actions, they become habits;
Watch your habits, they become your character;
Watch your character, it becomes your destiny.*

....

* These words are sometimes attributed to Mahatma Gandhi and sometimes to Lao Tzu. They appear in similar form in the Brihadaranyaka Upanishad (4.4.5) as "You are what your deep driving desire is. As your desire is, so is your will. As your will is, so is your deed. As your deed is, so is your destiny."

It's reasonable, I think, based on the testimony of so many who've traveled the path of meditation, to expect a beneficial shift such as a decrease in worry, reactivity, and stress in relationships. You might also begin to notice a tendency to feel more connected with others and with nature, or a stronger feeling of appreciation for people. Then again, it is equally reasonable to expect some disorientation and confusion to emerge as old patterns of interpersonal communication and relationship fail to provide the comfort they once did. As you continue to grow more connected to the silent witness of your own being, you may experience an accompanying sense of disconnection from unsupportable situations in your life, a loss of tolerance for that which drains you and leaves you feeling empty. Should this happen, you may experience some uncertainty about whether or not you should continue your practice. I remember a student came to me at the end of a ten-week class and asked me if in my opinion practicing meditation could make things worse. As he started to wake up to his inner life, he began also to notice the degree of *asleepness* in the company he was keeping and it was causing him to waver between the pull toward further waking up and retreating to old, comfortable ways of being. His friends were starting to worry about him because he was flipping between an old and a new version of his personality.

He explained that he felt vulnerable and challenged dealing with this because as his heart and mind were becoming awakened, unresolved issues finally had the opportunity to surface for attention, and he was experiencing unexpected emotions at inconvenient times. On the upside, he noticed he was finding deep, abiding satisfaction with things as simple as a wooden spoon while making dinner. However, this new fascination with inanimate objects and satisfaction with ordinary events wasn't contributing to the peace of mind among his friends and family who viewed his interest in meditation with misgiving as something strange and foreign. Over time, things settled, as they will, and he was able to look back at his journey and see that on one hand, his growing sense of his inner life helped him feel solid and awake, and on the other hand, this new version of himself left him feeling both impatient at how long things were taking and at the same time nervous that it was all going too fast.

Sometimes, and I pray this isn't the case for you, the discomfort of awakening through meditation practice is so great that some decide to go back to sleepwalking. The problem is, they discover soon enough, that the door they opened to wide-awake living can never again be fully closed. It tugs on our sleeve, beckoning us to wake up.

They may struggle with a pull between two worlds as life continues to open up and reveal how truly complex it is.

We are not alone. More and more people are having experiences like this. Whether we call it spiritual awakening or an increase in self-awareness, it is not uncommon anymore. In my opinion, to think that the spiritual experience is rare and reserved for others is a serious obstacle to our own progress. The experience of waking up is different for different people. For some, it comes like a blast of fireworks that lights up a night sky, and after the show they are dazzled and disoriented and wonder if they will ever regain it. For others, it's a progressive shift in awareness in which they slowly awaken to how their thoughts, words, and actions are connected. In whatever form it comes, it is generally the case that the world as we once understood it gives way to something that is unique to each individual and is very difficult to properly describe with words. And the changes that accompany awakening could also be so subtle that no one will know that you are no longer the *you* you used to be.

For those who have the fireworks version, the good news is that although the experience seems to fade and not fully return, I believe that it never quite leaves, and even the fact that we can recall it and describe it and long for it tells us of an enduring change that has taken place.

Author and Buddhist teacher Bruce Frantzis describes the possible change powerfully:

> When we can be fully present to our experiences, we see life as it is without filters, and we don't make excuses about why things should or shouldn't be different. We acknowledge the situation we find ourselves in and accept it. With acceptance of life as it is, we gain something else simultaneously—the ability to change. As long as we reject any situation we find ourselves in, we lose the ability to adapt. Eventually, if we can stay present long enough, we arrive at a point of neither accepting nor rejecting, and we can let everything just be.*

A Calm Mind

The 1997 movie *Contact* is about looking for, or listening for, extraterrestrial communication and finally discovering a signal from outer space. It's based on the novel with the same name by well-known astronomer Carl Sagan, who had an incredible way of explaining science to people like

....

* Bruce Frantzis, *Tao of Letting Go: Meditation for Modern Living* (Berkeley, Calif.: North Atlantic Books, 2009), p. 12.

me who need a little more help putting the pieces together. He had a way of reaching ordinary nonscience people so that they could understand and even become inspired by the vastness of the universe around us. Even though he was himself agnostic and is thought of as a freethinking skeptic, his work inspired me to be an awestruck believer in the great whatever-it-is. I'm grateful to him for that even though my almost religious reverence for creation may have been an unintended outcome of his beautiful work.

The opening sequence in *Contact* is one I often remember when I'm thinking about meditation and what I can expect from the practice. Inevitably, people who begin looking inward through meditation will start to ask themselves what I call the really, really big questions, such as "Why am I here?" "What is my purpose, if there is such a thing?" "What is Life?" The movie begins with a view pulling back from Earth, and as it does, we can hear several radio broadcasts coming from the various countries of the world, and the farther out we go into space, the further back in time the broadcasts go. I found the opening sequence engaging and disturbing as it reminded me of the really, really big questions. Eye-opening, and overwhelming, because I realize that there is so much going on in the airwaves of life that it can be challenging to figure out what is what, and what it means. With all this noise, could an outsider really know what a human being is? Sadly, maybe yes and quite possibly not at all, because none of us is represented by all of the messages and events of history, and yet at the same time we are a product of all of it.

It doesn't surprise me that the really, really big question "Who am I?" is so difficult to answer. Perhaps it is difficult because there is so much internal noise. Sometimes people report to me that up until the time they first became aware of that question, all they had to go on was the loud broadcasting of accumulated group-mind and history. Now, I'm not talking about radio waves floating out to space. I'm talking about the loud broadcast of messages that come from our culture, our fears and desires, our family histories, and then there is the pull from advertising, religion, and politicians all contributing a hefty influence on what you decide the answer to. "Who am I?" ought to be.

From time to time, I look in my e-mail spam filter to be certain that no good messages were incorrectly tagged as spam and dumped into the morass of information targeted at me. It is amazing what is in there. Messages about how to make yourself more attractive to others, to have a more satisfying sexual experience, to control your weight and appetite, schemes to get rich without working more than an hour or two, easy ways to get prescription drugs, and so on. Every time I look in there, I realize again that there is so much going on in the airwaves of life that it can be really challenging to figure out what is going on in me.

When I am asleep—and I don't mean at night, I mean when I am walking around, participating in the world, but numbed out by the avalanche of information and messages, so that I might as well be asleep—that is when I am more susceptible to the messages and more likely to take them at face value and eventually become shaped by them. To stay awake is to cultivate the inclination to look at it all with compassion and to evaluate, to the best of our ability, what is true and what is not.

Making It Up

I remember when I first encountered the publication *A Course in Miracles*,* I didn't at first get very far past the first five or six lessons in the workbook because of the impact they had on me and how they caused me to look into the world. The lessons asked me to question what I take to be real and to inquire into the roaring broadcast of life. The way I would summarize the first six lessons is this:

....

* *A Course in Miracles* (New York: Viking/Foundation for Inner Peace, 2007).

- Nothing I see means anything.
- I have given everything I see all the meaning that it has for me.
- I do not understand anything I see.
- These thoughts do not mean anything.
- I am never upset for the reason I think.
- I am upset because I see something that is not there.

That was interesting for me, to say the least, and I couldn't move through the lessons quickly. The questions left me sitting on my living room floor staring at a wall with amazement at my discovery of how very much of everything I was making up. Of course, I had been given some assistance in making it all up, I was using the roadmap provided by my culture, broadcast constantly on every channel, that informed me about when I should be upset, what I should want to be when I grow up, and how I would know when I was successful. I seemed to have a storehouse of solid information to back up the way I added meaning to everything, including what the right attitude toward work is, what is the correct way to believe, and so on. My head was so full that there wasn't space to ask the really, really big questions, until I began the practice of sitting, and in the quiet I felt more at ease in considering the questions:

"What am I?" "Why am I here?" "Is there a purpose?" "What is divinity?" It is in the quiet of the calm-mind that meditation provides that I was able to sit with these questions and others, without striving for a correct answer but rather just looking into the question.

In *A More Ardent Fire*,* Eknath Easwaran tells a story about his teaching in India in which he encounters two brothers in a class, both excellent soccer players but not particularly good academic students. During a good game, he noticed how present each boy was for what they were doing and suggested to them that if they could just concentrate in the same way during school, they would excel in their studies. Their answer was that they didn't know how they were being present during the game, because they didn't think about it in advance as something to switch on, rather their feet just did everything and they were present for the game.

Paradoxically it is like being present and at the same time not. It's not the same as mindlessly watching television, although I can see how that is useful too for relaxation. It is more like being engaged in whatever you're doing, but at the same time being an observer of what you are doing. It's as if you're participating, but the part of your

....

* Eknath Easwaran, *A More Ardent Fire: From Everyday Love to Love of God* (Tomales, Calif.: Nilgiri Press, 2000), p. 69.

mind that layers on meaning is not engaged in interpreting or evaluating.

Eknath Easwaran suggests that if you ask champion athletes, they will report something similar, that if their mind does step in and get involved in the process, the consequences would not be good, because now they would be engaged in projecting ideas of winning and losing, or possibly resurfacing snippets of conversations, and in all that activity, the gentle witnessing is obscured and mistakes begin to creep in. The quiet-mind that observes doesn't reason, plot, or plan. These activities have the effect of taking us out of the moment and cause us to reach into the future or past. The idea is to be in the activity of the game or whatever activity is before you. The idea is to be in your life as both spectator and participant.

The quiet-mind is the mind that lets the athlete, artist, musician, and you do your thing in the midst of the roar of information, uninhibited by the pressure of opinion and projected meaning. The quiet-mind makes clear-seeing accessible and brings aliveness with it. The loud influences and persuasive messages that come to us from family, friends, advertising, and religion ought not be discarded as garbage, but rather seen with compassion, sorted through, and evaluated. With compassion you can see that there is pressure to shape you, to influence you to want something.

You can notice the tendency of the group-mind to harness attention to self with compelling messages that you should always have what you want, always do what you want, and always get what you want, regardless of the cost to the world or to others. Whereas in the still-mind, it becomes difficult to detach from our connection to others and to our world; instead, we detach from the noise. When we begin to do that, my experience is that it allows us to be in the world in a gentle, compassionate, and powerful way.

> *When the mind is still, there is no self-will, no separateness, no sense of compulsion. We live in unity, and the natural expression of unity is love—not just love for one person or another, but love for all people, all life. This is our native state. It is not necessary to acquire anything to become loving: when all self-will is removed from the person, what remains is love.* *

Strip away everything and what remains is love. Here is how I work with the idea. I try to pay attention to when my mind is making up something. Then I look at that. I look especially for ideas that begin with the words "I am . . ."

....
* Easwaran, *A More Ardent Fire*, p. 72.

221

These arise at moments, for example, when I notice someone parked in two parking spaces instead of one. "I am annoyed." I try to remember and apply the lessons from *A Course in Miracles*, "Nothing I see means anything." The driver is trying to annoy me. "I have given everything I see all the meaning that it has for me." The driver does this because he doesn't care about others. "I do not understand anything I see." I am getting myself all worked up about this. "These thoughts do not mean anything." She doesn't respect me or other people. "I am never upset for the reason I think." This was intended purposefully. "I am upset because I see something that is not there."

It takes time to practice recognizing thoughts for what they are. As you become more skilled at questioning your mind, stillness increases and you may discover that there are a few basic themes that are repeating over and over again in your inner dialogue. Learning how to access the quiet in your mind requires patience and gentleness, because it can be wild in there, and things jump around. Like the opening sequence of *Contact*, there is a lot of content, and that can make it difficult to concentrate; so many snippets of interesting, scary, wonderful, frightening, lovely things to take in. Which one I should go with, you may wonder, and among those that are interesting, which ones are right for me to follow.

Try, and Try Again

The Bhagavad Gita is helpful in this regard, and when I read it, I detect playfulness in some of the instructions, a kind of tongue-in-cheek humor that for me acknowledges the paradoxes and enigmas of practicing. There is a part in the Bhagavad Gita in which God in the form of Krishna says to Prince Arjuna that there is a method that has worked for spiritual aspirants. I expected something direct, practical, and specific, and what Krishna gives instead is advice to try, and to keep on trying until success is achieved. When I read that, I smiled. It's too simple. Or is it? The word "try" in an archaic meaning of the word means to determine the truth of, or to find out to be correct by test or experience. To try to still the mind means to give it a chance and examine the results; to test it.

Many years ago, I hired a fitness trainer to coach me in getting in shape. After the first session, I never wanted to go back because of the aches I felt in places I didn't realize existed on the human body. I began to think, "How bad is it, being a little out of shape? I am, after all, getting older, and it's part of the journey." That to me is the roar of the group-mind and has to be accepted with compassion, but not necessarily listened to. Fortunately, with training your mind, you don't need to hire a consultant or purchase a special outfit or join an organization because you can begin right where you are with what you've got, by just being willing to try your mind, question what's in there, and discover if it is true. What I suspect will happen is that stillness will come to you and you won't have to force yourself to sit still. I suspect that in the process of watching your thoughts, you will discover what is underneath it all, or more accurately, what is underneath will come to you as your own wise, calm, nonreaching, nonclinging, nonfearing self.

I stuck it out with my trainer and can report—and it may not be good news—that like the mind, the body wants to go back to its old ways of comfort and convenience. But as I stayed with both physical and meditation programs, I noticed I had to convince myself less and less to do my work. When I got past that hurdle of showing up for the practices, things had a momentum of their own, subtleties were able to reveal themselves that simply weren't available because I was focused on my resistance to doing the work.

But what if, as it is asked in the Bhagavad Gita, you lack the will for such self-discipline? Krishna recommends that you try quieting your mind and fixing your thought on divinity as the best practice, but if you cannot do that, then learn to do so through the regular practice of meditation, and if you lack the will for such self-discipline, then practice selfless service and let everything you do be an act of worship. And, if you cannot do this, then practice being unattached to the results of your action, and do everything for something larger than your own life, because peace is the immediate result of surrendering attachment to outcomes. Krishna also describes the kind of adherents that he favors as being those who are not agitated by the world or agitating to the world, who neither run toward pleasant goals nor away from difficulties, but let things come and go as they happen; those who are not puffed up when praised, nor depressed when blamed or criticized, but who experience themselves as connected to all-that-is.

In other words, be gentle with yourself, and experiment with a practice that works with you and don't hesitate to adjust your course until you find your way.

FINAL WORDS

Meditation and spiritual practice have reacquainted me with something I think all people know instinctively from an early age, and that is that you and I are supposed to be here. It seems obvious, but for many, the innocent simplicity of that idea is forgotten after early cultural and religious conditioning, and we may begin to wonder if we are in the right place at all.

We are.

And sitting in simple stillness is when I remember most clearly that we are supposed to be here, feeling the deep, complex, and heart-opening experiences of belonging to life. Present-tense life is a soulful experience, one that we are meant to be engaged in, and delight in. Its present-tense beauty is easily missed when awareness is invested in other time zones. Life isn't something to be endured or survived, but to be witnessed compassionately with awe and wonder. Even those parts that seem incomprehensibly difficult, I am discovering. As with difficult thoughts that insert themselves into my meditation, when I can be as peaceful and accommodating with my challenges, they have the potential to reveal some hidden, if not somber, meaningfulness. Meditation has helped me lean into life's present moments instead of fleeing into moments of imagined futures, or fleeing from the past. Meditation reacquaints me regularly to be here, now.

I consider meditation to be the essential ingredient in my spiritual life. It helps me to appreciate being alive, enjoy my body, explore my mind, express my creativity, and most important, contribute to our world. It also helps me balance my reactive nature, and be kinder about those times when I completely forget, when I am inconsistent with my stated values. I'm far more forgiving with myself and others. Meditation has made me a more realistic person, one who sees how living a spiritual life takes courage, flexibility, listening, forgiveness, kindness, and a tremendous sense of humor.

Sitting in stillness has provided access to inner wisdom, and this access has prompted changes in my life that have been both wonderful and uncomfortable. I have had the feeling sometimes that I am in a constant "coming out" process with fewer places to hide the real me. I have had to learn to own my life, in the sense of taking responsibility for everything in it. By "life," I mean inner life. I have come to meet the one who is the master of my fate, the shaper of my destiny, and it is always the same one, the one who shapes your life and determines the difference between being not really unhappy, but not quite joyful. It is the same one who defines whether I am not quite bored, but not exactly engaged. That one is the "I" of me, or the "I" of you.

Through meditation, I have been shifting my attention from wherever it has been, and I shift a little more successfully every day toward a life in which I do, be, and express what is mine. Whether that means to contribute something to the world working better for others, or if it means consciously refraining from doing harm, or if it means I find peace in painting a watercolor no one will ever see, or something else, I am noticing my attraction toward a wholly lived life is increasing.

If you meditate, and maybe you already know this, you will slowly but surely disengage from the mass-believed concepts of what life, love, and happiness are about, and you will gradually become acquainted with your own inner wisdom, which you will come to call the truth. You will know it as true for you without ever needing to enroll anyone else into your way of thinking. You will will trust implicitly that what you have discovered is available to them below the surface of any sleepwalk-living they may be engaged in, just as it was for you.

In one of the classes I teach, we ask students to prepare their own memorial service and to write their own eulogy and deliver it. It is a tender and beautiful class experience in which students get to know themselves and each other in intimate and truly satisfying ways. The question of what it is that someone will say when they are eulogizing us is one that unlocks the door to a world of self-understanding. Will they say, "She was a kind woman"? Or, "He loved people." Or, "She followed her dreams." Or, "To be near him was to feel peace." Whatever they may say, it isn't necessarily the case that they will know that you came to be that way because you practiced. That you practice is deeply personal, and at the same time possibly your most profound contribution to friends, family, and the world, because of the great work practicing will accomplish in you.

ACKNOWLEDGMENTS

Thank you to my close friends, colleagues, and family members, in alphabetical order, William Abel, Mark Beaudry, Sherrie Corbett, Randall Friesen, Christopher Fritzsche, Chris Michaels, Cynthia Panaino, and Allan Yeager, who in their own unique ways endured, corrected, supported, and encouraged me.

Thank you to Joel Fotinos, Andrew Yackira, and the team at Tarcher/Penguin who guided me through the completion of the project.

Thank you to the students and teachers (I cannot always tell them apart) whose valuable questions and instructions through the years have helped keep my inquiry into the power of meditation alive and strong.

Thank you to the beautiful people of the Center for Spiritual Living, Santa Rosa, for giving me a career in which I can read, learn, practice, and share what I discover.

And thank you, reader, for being open to the possibility of discovering an ancient technique to access your inner power.

ABOUT THE AUTHOR

Edward Viljoen (pronounced full-YOON) is the Senior Minister at the Center for Spiritual Living in Santa Rosa, California. He is the author of the Kindle books *The Bhagavad-Gita for Beginners*, *The Science of Mind and Spirit for Beginners*; co-author (with Chris Michaels) of *Spirit Is Calling* and *Practice the Presence*; and co-author (with Joyce Duffala) of *Seeing Good at Work*. He lives in California.

MORE BOOKS IN TARCHER/
PENGUIN'S LIFE-CHANGING
"POWER OF" SERIES . . .

The Power of Kindness
by Piero Ferrucci

A stirring examination of a simple but profound concept. Piero Ferrucci, one of the world's most respected transpersonal psychologists, explores the many surprising facets of kindness and argues that it is this trait that will not only lead to our own individual happiness and the happiness of those around us, but will guide us in a world that has become cold, anxious, difficult, and frightening.

The Power of Giving
by Azim Jamal and Harvey McKinnon

A wealth of down-to-earth ideas, exercises, and real-life stories that reveal to each reader the unique gifts he or she has to give—including kindness, ideas, advice, attention, hope, and more—and the many ways you can benefit from giving them, from better health to better job prospects.

The Power of Receiving
by Amanda Owen

A new paradigm for the twenty-first century—a philosophy that values receiving as much as giving and demonstrates that giving is enhanced when receiving is embraced. With the formula: Believe + Receive = Achieve, *The Power of Receiving* presents a wholly original yet easily accessible road map for people to follow, showing readers how to restore balance to their overextended lives and attract the life they desire and deserve.

The Art of Uncertainty
by Dennis Merritt Jones

This book invites readers to consider an essential message: learning to love the unknown by staying present in the moment. If the difficulties of recent years have taught us anything—particularly those who "did everything right" and still saw it all fall apart—it's that none of us has as much control over our lives as we believe. The only thing we can control is our next thought.

If you enjoyed this book, visit

www.tarcherbooks.com

and sign up for Tarcher's e-newsletter to receive
special offers, giveaway promotions, and
information on hot upcoming releases.

TARCHER